CliffsNotes™

Crime and Punishment

By James L. Roberts, Ph.D.

IN THIS BOOK

- Learn about the Life and Background of the Author
- Preview an Introduction to the Novel
- Explore themes, style and language, and literary devices in the Critical Commentaries
- Delve into in-depth Character Analyses
- Gain an understanding of the novel with Critical Essays
- Reinforce what you learn with CliffsNotes Review
- Find additional information to further your study in CliffsNotes Resource Center and online at www.cliffsnotes.com

WILEY
Wiley Publishing, Inc.

About the Author

James L. Roberts, PhD. is a Professor Emeritus at the University of Nebraska.

Editorial

Senior Project Editor: Colleen Williams Esterline
Acquisitions Editor: Greg Tubach
Copy Editor: Colleen Williams Esterline
Glossary Editors: The editors and staff at Webster's New World™ Dictionaries
Editorial Administrator: Michelle Hacker

Production

Indexer: York Production Services, Inc.
Proofreader: York Production Services, Inc.
Wiley Indianapolis Composition Services

CliffsNotes™ *Crime and Punishment*

Published by:
Wiley Publishing, Inc.
111 River Street
Hoboken, NJ 07030
www.wiley.com

Copyright © 2001 Wiley Publishing, Inc., New York, New York
Library of Congress Control Number: 00-107259
ISBN: 978-0-764-58655-2
Printed in the United States of America
15 14 13 12 11 10 9 8
1O/TR/RQ/QT/IN
Published by Wiley Publishing, Inc., New York, NY
Published simultaneously in Canada

Table of Contents

How to Use This Book

This CliffsNotes study guide on Dostoevsky's *Crime and Punishment* supplements the original literary work, giving you background information about the author, an introduction to the work, a graphical character map, critical commentaries, expanded glossaries, and a comprehensive index, all for you to use as an educational tool that will allow you to better understand *Crime and Punishment*. This study guide was written with the assumption that you have read *Crime and Punishment*. Reading a literary work doesn't mean that you immediately grasp the major themes and devices used by the author; this study guide will help supplement your reading to be sure you get all you can from Dostoevsky's *Crime and Punishment*. CliffsNotes Review tests your comprehension of the original text and reinforces learning with questions and answers, practice projects, and more. For further information on Dostoevsky and *Crime and Punishment*, check out the CliffsNotes Resource Center.

CliffsNotes provides the following icons to highlight essential elements of particular interest:

Reveals the underlying themes in the work.

Helps you to more easily relate to or discover the depth of a character.

Uncovers elements such as setting, atmosphere, mystery, passion, violence, irony, symbolism, tragedy, foreshadowing, and satire.

Enables you to appreciate the nuances of words and phrases.

Don't Miss Our Web Site

Discover classic literature as well as modern-day treasures by visiting the CliffsNotes Web site at www.cliffsnotes.com. You can obtain a quick download of a CliffsNotes title, purchase a title in print form, browse our catalog, or view online samples.

LIFE AND BACKGROUND OF THE AUTHOR

The following abbreviated biography of Dostoevsky is provided so that you might become more familiar with his life and the historical times that possibly influenced his writing. Read this Life and Background of the Author section and recall it when reading Dostoevsky's *Crime and Punishment,* thinking of any thematic relationship between Dostoevsky's novel and his life.

Personal Background

Fyodor Mikhailovich Dostoevsky was born in 1821, the second of seven children, and lived until 1881. His father, an army doctor attached to the staff of a public hospital, was a stern and self-righteous man while his mother was the opposite—passive, kind, and generous—and perhaps this fact accounts for Dostoevsky's filling his novels with characters who seem to possess opposite extremes of temperament.

Dostoevsky's early education was in an army engineering school, where he was apparently bored with the dull routine and the unimaginative student life. He spent most of his time, therefore, dabbling in literary matters and in reading the latest authors; his penchant for literature was obsessive. And almost as obsessive was Dostoevsky's preoccupation with death, for while the young student was away at school, his father was killed by the serfs on his estate. This sudden and savage murder smoldered within the young Dostoevsky, and when he began to write, the subject of crime, and murder in particular, was present in every new publication. It is, of course, the central concern of *Crime and Punishment*. Dostoevsky was never free of the horrors of homicide and even at the end of his life, he chose to write of another violent death—the death of a father—as the basis for *The Brothers Karamazov*.

After spending two years in the army, Dostoevsky launched his literary career with *Poor Folk*, a novel that was an immediate and popular success and one highly acclaimed by the critics. Never before had a Russian author so thoroughly examined the psychological complexities of man's inner feelings and the intricate workings of the mind. Following *Poor Folk*, Dostoevsky's only important novel for many years was *The Double*, a short work dealing with a split personality and containing the genesis of *Crime and Punishment*.

Perhaps the most crucial years of Dostoevsky's melodramatic life occurred soon after the publication of *Poor Folk*. These years included some of the most active, changing phases in all of Russian history, and Dostoevsky had an unusually active role in this era of change. Using influences acquired with his literary achievements, he became involved in political intrigues of a questionable nature. He was, for example, deeply influenced by new and radical ideas that were entering Russia from the West, and he soon became affiliated with those who hoped to revolutionize Russia with all sorts of Western reforms. Dostoevsky published many articles concerning various political questions knowing full well that they were illegal and that all printing was controlled and censored by the government.

The rebellious writer and his friends were, of course, soon deemed treasonous revolutionaries and placed in prison. After nine months, a number of them, including Dostoevsky, were tried, found guilty, and condemned to be shot by a firing squad.

The entire group was accordingly assembled, all preparations were completed, and the victims were tied and blindfolded. Then, seconds before the shots were to be fired, a messenger from the Tsar arrived. A reprieve had been granted. Actually the Tsar had never intended that the men were to be shot; he merely used this cruel method to teach Dostoevsky and his friends a lesson. This harrowing encounter with death, however, haunted him for the rest of his life.

After the commutation of the death sentence, Dostoevsky was sent to Siberia and during the four years in prison there, he changed his entire outlook on life. During this time, in horrible living conditions, he began to re-examine his values. A total change occurred within the man. He experienced his first epileptic seizure and began to reject a heretofore blind acceptance of the new ideas that Russia was absorbing. He underwent a spiritual regeneration so profound that he emerged with a prophetic belief in the sacred mission of the Russian people. He believed that the salvation of the world was in the hands of the Russian people and that eventually Russia would rise to dominate the world. It was also in prison that Dostoevsky formulated his well-known theories about the necessity of suffering. Suffering became man's chief means of salvation.

Career Highlights

Dostoevsky married a young widow while still in exile. After his exile, he served four more years as an army private, was pardoned, and left Siberia to resume his literary career. He soon became one of the great spokesmen of Russia. Then in 1866, he published his first great masterpiece, *Crime and Punishment*.

After finishing *Crime and Punishment*, Dostoevsky married again and went abroad, hoping to find peace from numerous creditors and also hoping to begin a new novel. The peace of mind Dostoevsky longed for he never found; instead, he accumulated even more guilt in addition to his ever-mounting debts from gambling. The novel Dostoevsky composed abroad was *The Idiot*, the story of a wholly good and beautiful soul. In his notes, Dostoevsky sometimes called his hero "Prince Christ"; he hoped to create a man who could not hate and who was incapable of base sensuality. The novel is another of his masterpieces, a fascinating, intense study of the destructive power of good.

Dostoevsky's last novel, *The Brothers Karamazov*, was his great masterwork and is today considered a masterpiece of Western literature. Only a year after its publication, Dostoevsky was dead, but already he was acknowledged to be one of Russia's greatest writers.

INTRODUCTION TO THE NOVEL

The following Introduction section is provided solely as an educational tool and is not meant to replace the experience of your reading the novel. Read the Introduction and A Brief Synopsis to enhance your understanding of the novel and to prepare yourself for the critical thinking that should take place whenever you read any work of fiction or nonfiction. Keep the List of Characters and Character Map at hand so that as you read the original literary work, if you encounter a character about whom you're uncertain, you can refer to the List of Characters and Character Map to refresh your memory.

Introduction

In the nineteenth century, the western world moved away from the romanticism found in the works of Pushkin in Russia, Goethe in Germany, Hawthorne and Poe in America, and Wordsworth in England and moved in toward a modern realistic approach to literature. While the world was still reading popular romantic novels and love poems, Russia was leading a movement into the new realistic approach to literature. Dostoevsky was one of the forerunners of this movement, along with Gustave Flaubert in France and Mark Twain in America.

This movement can be seen in many ways, some from a very philosophical way and some in the most simple way. For example, in the romantic writings, the writer was concerned with the mysterious, the strange, and the bizarre. Edgar Allan Poe's famous short stories, such as "The Fall of the House of Usher" could be located in New England, Scotland, or many other places, and the story would be the same. Romantic literature seldom had any distinct landmarks and no reference to any external matters. In contrast, Dostoevsky is very careful to ground his novels in actual places. In *Crime and Punishment*, he is very exact in identifying the names of the streets, the bridge where Raskolnikov sees a woman attempting suicide, and so on. Students and editors have measured the number of feet between Raskolnikov's tiny room and the old pawnbroker's apartment and have discovered that Raskolnikov had made an accurate account of the distance—that is, he walked 730 paces in order to reach the old pawnbroker's apartment to commit the murder.

Dostoevsky was not only a chronicler of the exact physical surrounding, he was also writing subjects of modern concern. During the time that Dostoevsky was writing and publishing, the American public was reading about the romantic adventures of Hiawatha and Evangeline by Longfellow, stories that were set in some unrealistic and romantic distant past, or else the bizarre stories of Edgar Allen Poe. Dostoevsky established one of the precepts of modern realism was to present life as it actually was lived. This is exactly what Dostoevsky did from his earliest novels to his final masterpiece *The Brothers Karamazov*.

Dostoevsky was a prodigious reader and was well informed about the newest ideas and the most recent philosophical concepts of his time. His characters are driven by inner emotions that were just being investigated towards the end of his life. Sigmund Freud's investigations of the psychological states of one's mind were being published only after Dostoevsky had written many of his studies of the mental forces that drive a person to commit certain acts. Porfiry's investigations into the motives behind a crime and of the mental state of the criminal would not become an acceptable manner of investigation until sometime in the twentieth century. As a psychologist, Dostoevsky was well ahead of Freud. His descriptions of the inner emotions are psychologically realistic and true. Some are based on fact: for example, due to his involvement with writing and printing censored material, and subsequently, being condemned to death (see "Life and Background of the Author" above), Dostoevsky would often write about man's absolute despair.

Just prior to the publication of *Crime and Punishment*, Dostoevsky had published his short masterpiece *Notes from Underground*. A knowledge and understanding of this short novel is central to understanding most of Dostoevsky's novels. The Underground man (he is never named) begins his story by saying: "I am a sick man. . .I am a spiteful man. I am an unattractive man." This dirty, spiteful, human "louse" is still a human being, and it is Dostoevsky's first introduction to a human as a louse—such a one as Raskolnikov kills in *Crime and Punishment*.

The ideas expressed in *Notes from Underground* become central to all of Dostoevsky's later novels. As expressed in the Commentaries, Dostoevsky was writing partly about man's sense of freedom, the freedom to choose, to be able to have the right to step over obstacles. The right of man to have freedom and to be able to reject security in favor of the freedom to choose has its greatest expression in Dostoevsky's *The Brothers Karamazov*. In the scene where the Grand inquisitor confronts Jesus and says to Jesus that man prefers security to the freedom to choose that Jesus offers man, we have the greatest culmination of Dostoevsky's ideas upon freedom versus security.

At one point the Underground Man says that twice two makes four, this is a scientific fact, but man does not always function merely by scientific fact. For Dostoevsky, the rational part of a man's being is only one part of his makeup. That is, man is composed both of the rational (two times two does make four) and the irrational—"it would be nice to think sometimes that twice two makes five." This would be, in Dostoevsky's words, "a very charming idea also." The point is that if man functions solely as a rational being, then man's actions are always predictable. Thus,

Dostoevsky's point is that man's actions are *NOT* predictable. Raskolnikov will rationally stop a young dandy from having his way with a young girl and then suddenly decide it is none of his business, or he will tell his sister that he forbids her marriage and then contradict himself by saying "Marry whom you please." Likewise, there are men who are only happy when they suffer; thus, the man who falsely confesses to the murder of the old pawnbroker wants to suffer, particularly to suffer at the hands of authority.

One of the great ideas throughout all of Dostoevsky's fiction is that through suffering man can expiate all his sins and become more closely attuned with the basic elements of humanity. Thus in *Crime and Punishment*, we have Dostoevsky bowing down to Sonya because she represents the *sufferings of all humanity*. Both Sonya and his sister Dunya feel that when Raskolnikov takes up his suffering, he will be purified. Also, a person of great conscience will suffer from his transgressions, and as soon as the crime is committed, Raskolnikov suffers so greatly that he does become physically ill and is in a semi-coma for days.

Raskolnikov, both in his published article about crime and in his own actions, was involved in determining the mental states that affect the criminal. The concepts of psychology and even some of its later terminology were used by Raskolnikov and Porfiry. Examples abound as to Dostoevsky's use of modern psychological concepts. Porfiry's entire investigative technique involves his use of psychology to trap his victim, and Raskolnikov recognizes this and refers to it as a *cat and mouse* game.

In terms of world literature, Dostoevsky stands out as the greatest master of the realistic psychological novel and has yet to be equaled by any modern masters.

A Brief Synopsis

Raskolnikov, an impoverished student, conceives of himself as being an extraordinary young man and then formulates a theory whereby the extraordinary men of the world have a right to commit any crime if they have something of worth to offer humanity. To prove his theory, he murders an old, despicable pawnbroker and her half-sister who happened to come upon him suddenly. Immediately after the crime, he becomes ill and lies in his room semi-conscious for several days. When he recovers, he finds that a friend, Razumihkin, had looked for him. While he is

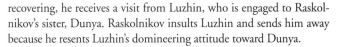

recovering, he receives a visit from Luzhin, who is engaged to Raskolnikov's sister, Dunya. Raskolnikov insults Luzhin and sends him away because he resents Luzhin's domineering attitude toward Dunya.

As soon as he can be about again, Raskolnikov goes out and reads about the crime in all the newspapers of the last few days. He meets an official from the police station and almost confesses the crime. He does go far enough in his ranting that the official becomes suspicious. Later, he witnesses the death of Marmeladov, a minor government official, who is struck by a carriage as he staggers across the street in a drunken stupor. Raskolnikov assists the man and leaves all his money to the destitute widow. When he returns to his room, he finds his mother and sister who have just arrived to prepare for the wedding with Luzhin. He denounces Luzhin and refuses to allow his sister to marry such a mean and nasty man. About the same time, Svidrigailov, Dunya's former employer, arrives in town and looks up Raskolnikov and asks for a meeting with Dunya. Previously Svidrigailov had attempted to seduce Dunya and when Raskolnikov had heard of it, he naturally formed a violent dislike for the man.

Raskolnikov hears that the police inspector, Porfiry, is interviewing all people who had ever had any business with the old pawnbroker. Therefore, he goes for an interview and leaves thinking that the police suspect him. Since he had met Sonya Marmeladov, the daughter of the dead man that he had helped, he goes to her and asks her to read to him from the Bible the story of Lazarus. He feels great sympathy with Sonya who had been forced into prostitution in order to support her family while her father drank constantly. In her suffering, she becomes a universal symbol for Raskolnikov. He promises to tell her who murdered the old pawnbroker and her sister who was a friend of Sonya's.

After another interview with Porfiry, Raskolnikov determines to confess to Sonya. He returns to her and during the confession, Svidrigailov is listening through the adjoining door. He uses this information to try to force Dunya to sleep with him. She refuses and he kills himself later in the night.

Porfiry informs Raskolnikov that he knows who murdered the pawnbroker. After talking with Sonya, Raskolnikov fully confesses to the murder and is sentenced to eight years in a Siberian prison. Sonya follows him, and with her help, Raskolnikov begins his regeneration.

List of Characters

Rodion Romanovitch Raskolnikov (Rodya, Rodenka, or Rodka) A poverty-stricken student who conceives of a theory of the "Ubermensch" or extraordinary man who has the right and/or obligation to trangress the laws of the ordinary man in order to give a *New Word* or idea to all of humanity. He uses this theory as a justification or rationalization to commit murder.

Sonya Marmeladov (Sofya Semyonovna Marmeladov) A quiet, modest, suffering prostitute who will become Raskolnikov's chief redemptive figure.

Porfiry Petrovitch An official of the investigating department who is in charge of the "crime."

Svidrigailov (Arkady Ivanovitch) A sensualist and vulgarian who asserts his own will in order to achieve his personal goals.

Dunya (Avdotya Romanovna Raskolnikov) Raskolnikov's devoted sister who was previously Svidrigailov's employee and who was propositioned by him.

Razumihkin (Dmitri Prokofitch) One of Raskolnikov's student friends who will become enamored of his sister Dunya.

Semyon Zakharovitch Marmeladov A dismissed government clerk who is an alcoholic.

Katerina Ivanovna Marmeladov Marmeladov's consumptive wife had been previously married to an army officer by whom she had three children.

Pulcheria Alexandrovna Raskolnikov Raskolnikov's mother who is frightened of her moody and intellectual son.

Alyona Ivanovna The sadistic and nasty moneylender whom Raskolnikov murders.

Lizaveta Ivanovna The mild, likable half sister to Alyona who is brutalized by her.

Polenka, Lyona, Kolya (Kolka) Katerina Ivanovna's children by a previous marriage. Sonya's greatest fear is that Polenka might have to enter into prostitution—Raskolnikov plagues her with this thought.

Marfa Petrovna Svidrigailov's wife who once assumed Dunya had designs on her husband.

Luzhin (Pyotr Petrovitch) A petty and miserly clerk in government who wants a poor person for his bride so that she will be indebted to him.

Lebezyater nikov (Andrey Semyonovitch) Luzhin's roommate who calls himself an "advanced liberal."

Praskovya Pavlovna Raskolnikov's shy and plump landlady.

Nastasya Praskovya Pavlovna's maid who befriends Raskolnikov and looks after him when he is ill.

Amalia Fyodorovna The Marmeladov's landlady who is particularly disliked by Katerina Ivanovna Marmeladov.

Kapernaumovs Sonya and Svidrigailov rent rooms from these rather depressed people.

Zossimov The doctor who cares for Raskolnikov during his illness.

Nikodim Fomitch A handsome police officer who was also at Marmeladov's death scene and reports this fact to Porfiry.

Zametov (Zamyotov), Alexander Gigorevitch The chief
clerk at the police station.

Ilya Petrovitch A loud and somewhat overbearing police official
to whom Raskolnikov makes his confession when there was no one
else to confess to.

Nikolay (Milkolka) and Dmitri (Mitka) The painters who
were working in the flat below the pawnbroker's flat at the time of
the crime.

Russian Names

The middle name of all male characters end in "ovitch" and of all
female characters in "ovna." This ending simply means "son of" or
"daughter of" the father whose first name is converted into their middle name and is called a patronymic. For example, Rodya and Dunya's
father was named Roman Raskolnikov. Thus, Rodya's middle name
Rodion Romanovitch means son of Roman and Dunya's middle name,
Avdotya Romanovna, means daughter of Roman.

A Note on Pronunciation

If the reader will remember to give strong stress to the syllable
marked with an accent in this list, to give the vowels their "continen-
tal" value, and pronounce the consonants as in English, a rough approx-
imation to the Russian pronunciation will be obtained. The consonant
"kh" sounds rather like the Scottish "ch" in "loch"; the "zh" represents
a sound like "s" in "measure"; and the final "v" is pronounced "f."

`Rodion Ro`manovitch Ras`kolnikov: "raskol"=schism or split.

Svidri`gailov

Razu`mikhin: "razum"=reason or common sense.

Marme`ladov: "marmelad"= jam or jelly.

Al`yona I`vanovna

Character Map

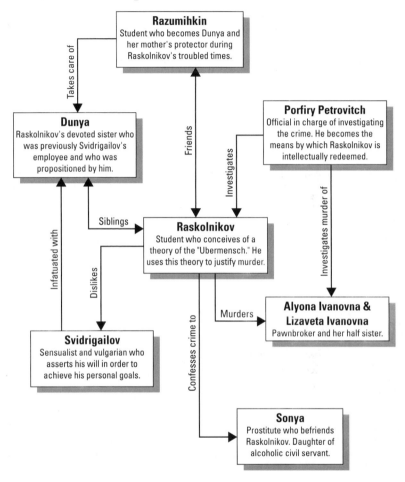

CRITICAL COMMENTARIES

The sections that follow provide great tools for supplementing your reading of *Crime and Punishment*. First, in order to enhance your understanding of and enjoyment from reading, we provide quick summaries in case you have difficulty when you read the original literary work. Each summary is followed by commentary: literary devices, character analyses, themes, and so on. Keep in mind that the interpretations here are solely those of the author of this study guide and are used to jumpstart your thinking about the work. No single interpretation of a complex work like *Crime and Punishment* is infallible or exhaustive, and you'll likely find that you interpret portions of the work differently from the author of this study guide. Read the original work and determine your own interpretations, referring to these Notes for supplemental meanings only.

Part One
Chapter 1

Summary

On a hot and sultry day in July, Rodion Romanovitch Raskolnikov, a young student, slips past his landlady to whom he is heavily in debt, and roams aimlessly towards an old and despicable pawnbroker, Alyona Ivanovna. He has cut himself off from everyone and furthermore shrinks from any type of human conduct. His little cupboard of a room, his debts, and his crushing poverty depress him to the point of rendering him incapable of attending classes or tutoring his own students.

On the way to the pawnbroker's, he simply cannot believe that he is going to perform some loathsome action. He also realizes that his thoughts are confused, partly because he had eaten practically nothing for two days. Even though he was a strikingly handsome young man, he dresses so wretchedly in rags that no one would notice his secretive behavior.

It was not far to the pawnbroker's house—"exactly seven hundred and thirty" paces. Upon arriving, he seems to be disgusted with the entire proceedings and finds his plans to be loathsome and degrading. The old pawnbroker is cautious about opening the door, and when she does, she appears dried up and very old, with sharp, malicious eyes and nasty grease in her hair. Raskolnikov tells her he has something else to pawn, and they haggle over the price, but he has to accept her offer because "he had nowhere else to turn." As he leaves, he tells her that he has something more valuable to pawn and he will bring it later. He leaves in a state of extreme agitation.

Commentary

In any novel as great as *Crime and Punishment*, the details of the early or introductory chapters will become central to the interpretation of the entire novel. In this first chapter, Raskolnikov is seen isolated from everyone; later, he even feels uncomfortable around his mother and sister. And in the Epilogue when Raskolnikov is in prison in Siberia, he feels isolated and estranged from his fellow prisoners: ". . . he felt that terrible unbridgeable chasm which lay between him and the others. . .as if he and they belonged to different races." Both in this first chapter and the Epilogue, Raskolnikov avoided everyone. Throughout the novel he will begin a conversation with an individual and suddenly without any reason, he will leave and isolate himself further.

This first chapter also emphasizes his extreme poverty and his small, cramped apartment. Often during the novel, these physical matters will be used to explain his crimes and his sick frightened feelings that are attributed to the squalor of his room and his lack of food.

In contrast to his physical surroundings, his personal appearance is exceptional; even though he is clothed in rags, he is still exceptionally handsome, slim, "well-built with beautiful dark eyes and dark brown hair." Too often, even today, illustrators often depict Raskolnikov as physically depraved and/or deformed—a vicious Mr. Hyde or a horrible misfit. Unlike other great writers, such as Dickens, whose evil characters are described in frightful terms, Dostoevsky does just the opposite—he presents Raskolnikov as physically attractive so as to prevent any possible view that the ugliness of his crime is influenced by a physical deformity. In contrast, the physical beauty of the character contrasts significantly with the ugliness of the crime.

Ultimately, Raskolnikov will emerge as a dual character, fluctuating between two extremes. For example, he is making such careful preparations for the crime, even going so far as to count the number of paces from his room to Alyona Ivanovna's apartment. Yet in the very midst of his careful preparation, he is alternately disturbed by the loathsomeness and ugliness of the crime and that his entire plan is atrocious and degrading. But even with these repulsive thoughts, he continues to prepare for the murder.

Furthermore, his plans have not yet been finalized. He knows of his crime only in theory, a fact that will later become central to his redemption when he attempts to explain his reasons to Sonya at the end of the novel. Consequently, the reader must be prepared for opposite reactions occupying Raskolnikov's mind, and what would seem an inconsistency elsewhere is here used to explain his dual (or split) personality. His visit to Alyona Ivanovna's shows both his repulsion to his plan and his preparations for its execution.

Glossary

Here and in the following chapters, difficult words and phrases, as well as allusions and historical references are explained.

Kameny Bridge A bridge close to the Hay Market square that leads from Raskolnikov's room to Alyona Ivanova's apartment. In reality, Dostoevsky did not name this bridge; he only referred to it as "K-----Bridge. An early student or editor identified it incorrectly as Kameny Bridge, but to be historically correct, to get from Raskolnikov's tiny room to Alyona's apartment, one crosses over the Kokushkin Bridge. All the streets and building landmarks are very accurate. Dostoevsky was very careful in his realistic descriptions. For example, students have measured the distance from Raskolnikov's room to the pawnbroker's flat, and it is actually about 730 paces, the same as Raskolnikov counted.

Hay Market A section of the city best known for its low and bohemian life. Around the square are cheap student housings such as Raskolnikov's room and also houses of prostitution that were easily accessible to Sonya. Drunks such as Marmelodov would also congregate here in the square. See Map, Item 4.

Sadovaya Street A street somewhat off the main Hay Market square and parallel to the canal. It was through here that Raskolnikov made his way to the pawnbroker.

rouble The main Russian monetary unit. At the time of the novel, the rouble consisted of 100 copeks and was worth approximately 50 cents. Thus when Raskolnikov pawns his watch for 1½ roubles, he received approximately 75 cents.

vodka Russian alcoholic beverage now very popular in the United States and around the world. It is a clear liquid made essentially from fermented potatoes.

Part One
Chapter 2

Summary

At the end of the last chapter, Raskolnikov notices an apparently disturbed person in the tavern drinking. After his visit with Alyona Ivanovna, he feels the need of a drink, and the lonely man begins a conversation with him. He identifies himself as Semyon Marmeladov, a clerk in the Civil Service. He has neither undressed nor washed for five days. His greasy red hands were dirty, his nails filthy, and his clothes disreputable.

Marmeladov spills out his entire recent history, telling how he had been in government service but had lost his position because of alcoholism. However, he had recently been reinstated as a clerk in a government office, but as of now, he has been drinking constantly for five days and is now afraid to go home. He tells of his marriage to Katerina Ivanovna, a widow of a higher social class and a mother of three young children who married him out of destitution. He also reveals that he has a daughter Sonya who has entered into prostitution because there was no other way to feed the family. He stole the money his daughter earned from prostitution to pay for his five-day binge. He asks Raskolnikov "Can you say with conviction that I am not a swine?"

He asks Raskolnikov if he knows what it is like to have absolutely no place to turn to, to be in utter despair and to suffer without recourse to any action. He took Sonya's last 30 kopecks to buy drinks. He is scared to go home because Katerina will beat him and he deserves it.

Raskolnikov, who has wanted to leave, decides to help Marmeladov home where he sees the abject poverty that he, Katerina, and the three children live in. After witnessing a horrible scene between Marmeladov and Katerina, he scrapes through his pockets and leaves them some of his scant money.

Commentary

The introduction of Marmeladov at this point is central to Raskolnikov's theories. He has just left a woman (Alyona Ivanovna) who is filthy, greasy, and lives the life of a "louse"; he is repulsed by her and plans to murder her. Yet, here he meets Marmeladov who is also filthy, greasy, with dirty hands and is a horrible, abject creature who has allowed his own daughter to enter prostitution so as to help support his drinking habits; yet rather than seeing him as a "louse," the opposite feelings are evoked in Raskolnikov—he responds with sympathy and compassion to this outwardly useless creature.

Character Insight

This meeting with Marmeladov this early in the novel establishes Raskolnikov's dual personality. Throughout the novel, we should remember that Raskolnikov functions either as a warm, compassionate, and humane individual willing to help the downtrodden, or else as a cold, detached, intellectual being who must stand apart from others in order to justify his theories of the *Ubermensch*. At the beginning of Chapter 2, he has avoided all society of late but after his meeting with the pawnbroker (Alyona Ivanovna), he has a desire to embrace humanity. And his humanitarian impulses cause him to leave all (or most) of his scarce money to Katerina, but almost immediately, he changes his mind and "would have gone back."

The meeting with Marmeladov is also important in establishing future relationships. First, Marmeladov's narration introduces Sonya and the entire Marmeladov family. It prepares Raskolnikov to look upon Sonya as a victim and see in Marmeladov's own sufferings the sufferings of Sonya. He is attracted to her because of her suffering. Then, at the end of the novel just before his confession, he acknowledges his attraction to her because she represents "the suffering of all humanity."

Theme

Marmeladov's story also reflects Raskolnikov's own personal condition. The discussion of hopelessness, "when one has no one, nowhere else one can go," becomes one of the dominant motifs throughout the rest of the novel. This discussion reoccurs later as Raskolnikov is forced to consider the hopelessness of his own life. After the actual murder, Raskolnikov remembers Marmeladov's impassioned cry of "having absolutely no where to go."

Finally, Marmeladov's story stresses the alcoholic as a human being whose family is starving while he drinks, whose daughter had to enter into prostitution in order to support the starving family, and whose life has been one of degradation. Since Raskolnikov's murder will be based partially on the rationale that certain people fit into a category of being a "louse," this story should indicate to Raskolnikov that his theory should apply directly to Marmeladov, especially when Marmeladov cries out, "Dare you assert that I am not a pig?" But rather than despising Marmeladov as a louse (or a pig), Raskolnikov feels great sympathy for him and for his suffering, thus contradicting his own theory, and making him doubt the validity of his theory: "What if man is not really a scoundrel. . .then all the rest is prejudice."

Glossary

Civil Service People who worked in some aspect of the government were known as being in the civil service. They were ranked from 1-14, with 14 being at the bottom, such as a custodian, and the top being an administrator.

titular counsellor Marmeladov's title is that of the ninth rank. It is some one above that of custodian but not of a very high rank.

latest ideas Due to his frequent travels to Germany, Dostoevsky was familiar with the latest thinking in Western Europe. Many of Mr. Lebezyatnikov's ideas are found in John Stuart Mill's *Principles of Political Economy*, recently published in St Petersburg.

street walker A street walker is a prostitute who solicits her customers by walking the streets.

yellow passport or yellow ticket Prostitutes in Russia and most European countries were required to register with the police and carry a permit, that is, a yellow identity card.

the shawl dance This dance would be one learned in a boarding school for young ladies, especially those educated in socially desirable "finishing schools." It indicates that Katerina Ivanovna was of a superior class to her husband, Marmeladov.

Lewes' Physiology English author George Lewes (1817-78) of *The Physiology of Every-day Life*, which was available in Russian in 1861 and was very popular with the liberals in Russia.

Part One
Chapter 3

Summary

The next day, Raskolnikov awakens in his dirty cubbyhole of a room, feeling disgusted with his slovenly and degraded manner of living. He withdraws from human contact but still suffers. Nastasya, the servant meant to look after him, tells him that the landlady, Praskovya Pavlovna, is going to report him to the police because he has not paid his back rent. She also brings him a long letter from his mother.

When Nastasya leaves, he kisses his mother's letter and with trembling hands, he reverently opens it. His mother, Pulcheria Alexandrovna, writes of her abiding love for him and that his sister, Dunya, has been working in the Svidrigailov household as a governess. Unfortunately, Svidrigailov, a well-known sensualist, formed an intense attachment for Dunya and made unwarranted overtures and improper advances, including trying to persuade her to run away with him. The wife, Marfa Petrovna, overhears part of a conversation and believes that the attachment is all Dunya's fault even though she is fully aware of her husband's sensual propensities. Furthermore, Marfa spreads the lie all through the countryside. Later, Svidrigailov corrects her and even shows her a letter reprimanding him for his improper advances and admonishing him to be faithful to his wife. Upon discovering her mistake, once again Marfa Petrovna goes about the countryside showing the letter and proclaiming Dunya's innocence and goodness.

At this time, Marfa Petrovna had a kinsman, Pyotr Petrovitch Luzhin, visiting her who wanted a wife. He is searching for a poor wife with a sound reputation who is without a dowry so that his wife will be always indebted to him for his generosity. Thus he proposes to Dunya, who has accepted him.

Finally, Pulcheria Alexandrovna tells her son that both she and Dunya will soon be in St. Petersburg so as to be with Luzhin who will find them proper living quarters, and she promises to send Raskolnikov more money as soon as she can borrow it.

Commentary

This chapter provides us again with many small details that will later play an important role. For example, the description of his room, small and cramped, will later be used as one of the reasons for his mental breakdown and will be correlated with his search for clean air and freedom. Also, the servant, Nastasya, tells him that his landlady is going to go to the police about his back rent and debts. Ironically, Raskolnikov forgets this and when the police summons arrive the day after the murder, he immediately thinks that his crime has been discovered.

One should note that the sentimentality that Raskolnikov experiences in the receipt of his mother's letter and the love and the compassion it evokes does not conform to that of the cold, rational Ubermensch.

The letter conveys many important ideas that will influence later actions. First, he hears of Svidrigailov's behavior and propositions to his sister Dunya. Thus, before he ever meets Svidrigailov, he has formed a very negative opinion of him. He hears that Svidrigailov made vulgar propositions to her and that he insulted and frightened her. Thus Raskolnikov is prepared to dislike Svidrigailov before he ever meets him.

Secondly, he hears about Dunya's engagement to Luzhin, who wants a wife who will be subservient, obedient to his authority, and always indebted to him. Raskolnikov recognizes that Luzhin is a petty, selfish, and egocentric person, and subsequent events will prove that he is correct in his evaluation of Luzhin.

Finally, Pulcheria Alexandrovna explains their dire financial situation and their need for the bare necessities in arriving in St. Petersburg, but she hopes to squeeze 25 to 30 rubles to send to Raskolnikov. This money, which he receives and subsequently gives to the Marmeladov family, will become a central issue during the remainder of the novel.

Part One
Chapter 4

Summary

Upon finishing the letter, Raskolnikov resolves that Dunya will never sacrifice herself by marrying Luzhin, which she is doing only to be able to help him. He adamantly refuses such a sacrifice by saying, "While I live, this marriage will never take place."

Furthermore, he sees Luzhin as a mean and stingy person who would allow his fiancée and her mother ride in a peasant's cart for "seventeen versts" (around 12 miles) and to travel in third class accommodations on the train. After he considers Luzhin's entire proposal, Raskolnikov declares that "I will not have your [Dunya's] sacrifice, I will not have it. ..It shall not be, while I live, it shall not, it shall not! I will not accept it!" However, he has nowhere to turn to prevent such a disgraceful liaison.

While thinking about Dunya's plight, he observes a young 15-year-old girl staggering down the street as though she were either drunk or drugged. This young girl is being followed by a "foppish" and plump man; the man's intentions towards the young girl are obvious. Raskolnikov interferes and accosts the dandy. The police arrive and they get the girl into a cab; Raskolnikov offers his last 20 kopecks for the cab, but then "at this moment an instantaneous revulsion of feeling" causes him to reverse himself. He decides that he is interfering in something that does not concern him: "What does it matter. . .Let him [the dandy] amuse himself [with the girl]." He leaves resenting that he has lost his last 20 kopecks. "How dared I give away those twenty copecks? Were they mine to give?"

At the end of the chapter, he decides to visit Razumihkin, one of his best friends of times past, whom he has not seen in about four months.

Commentary

Raskolnikov is deeply offended by Luzhin's offer of marriage because he views Dunya as sacrificing herself to benefit him, and he cannot stand the idea of someone making such a sacrifice for him.

He makes a comparison between his sister's sacrifice to help her family and Sonya's sacrifice to help her family. He wonders if Dunya's marriage to Luzhin is not also a type of prostitution and may even be worse because Sonya's was for necessity and Dunya's could be for convenience.

The parallel between the two sacrifices troubles Raskolnikov because he can do nothing about them. This brings about the reoccurrence of the "Do you understand, sir, do you understand what it means when you have absolutely no where to turn?" theme. This parallel deeply troubles him because his present situation is also desperate and hopeless. He feels strongly that Dunya is sacrificing herself, but he can do nothing to alleviate the situation or prevent it.

Raskolnikov is deeply disturbed when he encounters the young girl, who has been abused and who is being followed by a man with evil designs upon her. This scene prompts the humanitarian side of his character into performing an act of protection. In his attempt to protect the girl, Raskolnikov calls the man a "Svidrigailov," thus making this name into the embodiment of depraved sensuality.

Raskolnikov's humanistic and compassionate nature is further revealed in his attempts to protect the young girl. He gives her almost all of his scarce money in order to send for a cab. The question arises: Would he have been so protective of the young girl if he had not just received the letter from his mother? Immediately after trying to help the young girl, he suddenly reverses himself and says "let them be." That is, suddenly, the cold, intellectual Ubermensch aspect of his personality takes over, and Raskolnikov maintains that such trivial happenings do not concern him—that he is too far above or removed to be involved. Carried further, he also should not be concerned with what happens to Dunya or Sonya, that is, if he is the true Ubermensch.

At the end, Raskolnikov's unexpected desire to see Razumihkin, his logical and rational friend, is caused by his awful feeling that he has "no where to turn."

Part One
Chapter 5

Summary

Before he reaches Razumihkin's place, Raskolnikov changes his mind but promises that he will go the "the day after, when that is over and done with," but then in despair he wonders if it will really happen. It frightens him so much that he goes into a tavern and has a glass of vodka. Since he was unaccustomed to alcohol, he walks unsteadily to a park and immediately goes to sleep.

He dreams that he is back in his childhood, seven years old, and as he is walking with his father, he sees a drunken peasant trying to make his old horse pull a heavy wagon full of people. When the crowd laughs at him and the ridiculous spectacle, the peasant gets angry and begins beating the old, feeble horse. He beats so ferociously that others join in the "fun." Finally they begin to use crowbars and iron shafts. The old horse at first tries to resist, but soon it falls down dead. The boy in the dream, feeling great compassion for the stricken and dead mare, throws his arms around the beast and kisses it. All through the dream the peasant owner is screaming that the mare was his and he had a right to do whatever he wanted to with her.

Upon awakening from the dream, Raskolnikov renounces that "accursed dream of mine" and wonders in horror: "Is it possible that I really shall take an axe and strike her on the head, smash open her skull . . . God, is it possible?" He then ". . .renounces this accursed fantasy of mine" because he will never summon up enough resolution to do it.

However, as he walks through the Hay Market, he overhears a conversation between tradespeople and Lizaveta Ivanovna, the half sister to the old pawnbroker, that on the next night "at seven o'clock in the evening the old woman would be at home alone."

Commentary

All through these early scenes Raskolnikov is somewhat feverish. Throughout the crime, he is not himself, and his irrational acts can be accredited to his illness. Ultimately, criminal theories suggest that the criminal is often sick when the crime is committed, and this theory will be used to alleviate Raskolnikov's guilt.

When Raskolnikov goes to sleep in the park, Dostoevsky lets us know that "A sick man's dreams are often extraordinarily distinct and vivid and extremely life-like. A scene may be composed of the most unnatural and incongruous elements, but the setting and the presentation are so plausible, the details so subtle, so unexpected, so artistically in harmony with the whole picture, that the dreamer could not invent them for himself in his waking state. Such morbid dreams always make a strong impression on the dreamer's already disturbed and excited nerves, and are remembered for a long time."

Thus, Dostoevsky is announcing to the reader that Raskolnikov's dream now and later will have special meaning to him and thus all the dreams are symbolic in one way or another.

When Raskolnikov awakens, he wonders if he can actually "take an axe. . .split her skull open. . .tread in the sticky warm blood. . .[and] hide." He ends by renouncing "that accursed dream of mine," thus symbolically rejecting his plan to murder Alyona Ivanovna. In the dream, Raskolnikov shows his dual nature at work. He is both the peasant Mikolka who cruelly beats the horse to death and also the boy who feels great compassion for the suffering horse. Thus, the waking Raskolnikov rejects the Mikolka aspect of his nature by renouncing the dream.

Other ideas developed later are present in the dream. The idea of property being the responsibility of the owner is touched upon. This relates to the pawnbroker's immense amount of property and the right to dispense with it as she pleases; even if she "wastes" it on monks chanting prayers for the dead, it is nevertheless her property. The idea of the innocent suffering as the horse must suffer is implicit. The horse has been interpreted as being "mother Russia" since later when Raskolnikov confesses, Sonya tells him to bow down and kiss the earth of mother Russia that he has defiled.

After the dream, the overheard conversation reveals that Lizaveta will be absent at 7:00 the next night. This forces Raskolnikov to consider it a perfect opportunity to commit the crime. Later Raskolnikov will attempt to justify the idea of the crime and maintain only that he executed it before the idea was completely formulated. But at this point, the destitute poverty, the emotional letter from his mother, and the favorable circumstance of Alyona Ivanovna's being alone will combine to push the actual act into immediate execution.

Glossary

icon An image or picture of Jesus, Mary, a saint, etc., venerated as sacred.

Holy Mother of Kazan This refers to an icon of the Virgin Mary, which was kept in the Kazan Cathedral in St. Petersburg. This is one of the most universally admired of all Russian icons.

Golgotha The place where Jesus was crucified.

Schilleresque This refers to the romantic heroes found in the writing of the German poet Schiller who wrote about beautiful sensitive souls.

Schleswig-Holstein Prussia, Denmark, and Austria were fighting a war over this land during the composition of *Crime and Punishment.* It implies a refusal to give up something of importance.

Vasilyevsky Ostrov This is not important except to show how grounded in reality is this novel. St. Petersburg was built on a marshy land and there are many islands in and around it.

dacha In Russia, a country house or cottage used as a vacation retreat.

Pushkin and Turgenev Aleksandr Sergeyevich Pushkin [1799-1837] is considered the father of Russian literature, and his home was outside of St. Petersburg. Ivan Sergeyevich Turgenev was a contemporary of Dostoevsky, and his novels were very popular.

Part One
Chapter 6

Summary

Raskolnikov remembers that Lizaveta has the appointment with the tradespeople because she acts as a go-between for impoverished families forced to sell their goods. He then remembers that he had the address of Alyona Ivanovna from a fellow student and even before he went to see her he had "felt an irresistible dislike for her."

While he is thinking about how obnoxious the pawnbroker is, he overhears a conversation between two young officers who had recently had business with her; they were enumerating all of her horrible flaws. Alyona Ivanovna is spiteful, cranky, and hateful. She charges an exorbitant usurious, interest rate (five to seven percent), is sadistic, and beats her half sister, Lizaveta Ivanovna. She greedily forecloses if one is even one day late, causing poor people to lose valuable property.

Raskolnikov hears the two officers justifying a proposition that the old woman was a detriment to society because actively causes harm and destroys the lives of innocent people by her usury. On the other hand, a person could kill her and use the money to save "scores of families. . . from beggary, from decay, from ruin and corruption." Would not thousands of good deeds wipe out one small transgression? The supposition ends when one of the officers asks the other: "Would you kill the old woman with your own hands?" Both agree that they would not, and that is the end of it.

After recalling this conversation, Raskolnikov begins to make preparations by sewing a noose into his overcoat and wrapping the pledge securely. He goes to steal the axe, but Nastasya, the servant, is sitting in the door. He takes an axe from the porter. These preparations delay him and it is 7:30 p.m. before he reaches the pawnbroker's. As he arrives, he notes that there is an empty flat under the pawnbroker's and workers are in there painting it. He climbs to Alyona Ivanovna's flat and rings the doorbell several times before she opens the door.

Commentary

The conversation Raskolnikov overheard six weeks ago is central to his justification for murdering such a person as Alyona Ivanovna. This conversation occurred at the same time that Raskolnikov was independently considering the same ideas. These ideas are not Raskolnikov's, nor Dostoevsky's, nor those of the two officers: Instead they are a synthesis of the German philosopher, Hegel (Georg Wilhelm Friedrich Hegel, 1770-1830—see CliffsNotes Resource Center for further information).

The thesis of Hegelianism that applies here is an altruistic one in that (1) the old pawnbroker is an active, "harmful thing" and her murder will remove blight upon society. (2) This old pawnbroker has actually been involved in evil matters. (3) Her considerable money, rather than being wasted in a monastery on useless prayers for her horrible soul, can be used to save multiple families from destitution. (4) The person who murders her can then use the money and devote himself "to the service of humanity and the good of all." Therefore, "one tiny crime would be wiped out by thousands of good deeds." The Hegelian antithesis is very simple; that is, who will do the actual killing? If no one is willing to perform this murder, then "there's no justice about it."

Even though Raskolnikov had already been considering these ideas some six weeks ago, he has concerned himself only with the general outlines of his plan and has not worked out details. Therefore, his difficulty later occurs because he "put off trifling details, until he could believe in it all." Thus, he is forced to commit the murder before he has completely resolved all the details.

Raskolnikov's thoughts about crime and psychology reveal his theory that the failure of any crime lies not so much in the impossibility of concealing the crime, as in the criminal himself. "Every criminal, at the moment of the crime, is subject to a collapse of will-power and reason. . . ." Thus, later, Raskolnikov, after murdering Alyona, has a failure of will when he leaves the apartment door wide open, allowing Lizaveta to enter and forcing Raskolnikov to kill her also, and when he arrives at the pawnbroker's a half an hour late.

Finally, the reader should keep in mind that painters are in the flat below; and later Raskolnikov will faint at the smell of paint. There is also an interminably long ringing sound of the bell—a sound that returns to him in his illness.

Part One
Chapter 7

Summary

As soon as the door was opened a crack, Raskolnikov forced his way into the pawnbroker's. She is frightened, and he gives her the pledge that he had wrapped so carefully, telling her that it is a silver cigarette case. As she laboriously unwraps the package, he removes the axe and, while her back is turned, he hits her with the butt end of the axe. He then strikes her again and again with the blunt end of the axe. Very carefully, he lays the axe down by the body and begins to search through her pockets for keys.

While searching for the keys, he notices that Alyona Ivanovna wears two crosses, one of cypress wood and one of copper. He then finds some keys and a small leather purse stuffed very full and he takes them. As he searches the rooms, he finds all sorts of gold and silver items, but he suddenly hears footsteps in the entranceway. He discovers Lizaveta standing over her murdered half sister. Raskolnikov immediately takes the axe and with Lizaveta staring at him in utter horror, he strikes her with one heavy blow "with the sharp edge just on the skull and splits at one blow all the top of her head." This "second unpremeditated murder" makes him want to completely abandon the entire project. After the second murder, he begins to think of confessing and immediately begins to cleanse the blood from his axe, hands, and clothes.

As he is ready to leave, the doorbell rings. Two individuals wait outside for their appointments with Alyona Ivanovna. As they try the door, they realize that it is locked from the inside. One leaves to go get the porter and then when the other leaves for a moment, Raskolnikov slips out and hides in the empty, newly painted room just below the pawnbroker's flat. When the murder is discovered, he slips out unnoticed and returns to his own room, where he replaces the axe in the porter's lodge and then falls into a state bordering on unconsciousness.

Commentary

Part One ends with the murder of Alyona. But in the dual murder scene, note that Alyona is murdered with the blunt side of the axe and as though one stroke were not enough to kill her, he then bludgeons the body with further strokes. In contrast, the murder of Lizaveta is quickly finished by a swift stroke of the sharp side of the axe. In this dual murder, he has killed one person who is mean, wicked, and cold (Alyona) and the murder was premeditated so as to prove a theory to himself. In the second murder, Lizaveta, who is warm, friendly, humane, gentle, and compassionate is instantaneously killed and her murder was not premeditated. Thus in a figurative manner, the two murders represent the two aspects of Raskolnikov's character. The importance here is that later Raskolnikov seldom thinks of the murder of Lizaveta but is troubled about the murder of Alyona because the death of the old louse is directly correlated to the validity of his theories, and Lizaveta's murder was accidental.

As soon as he completes the murder and as he is standing in the midst of the carnage, his first thought is "to abandon everything" and "to give himself up." This is the first of many thoughts of confession that will continue until the actual confession at the end of Part Five.

Covered with blood, he notices a bucket half full of water and he begins to wash his hands and the axe. This elaborate cleansing ritual foreshadows his future redemption and salvation.

When Raskolnikov is trapped by two people who have independently arrived at about the same time and as they are determinedly and incessantly ringing the doorbell, he thinks of confession, motivated by the horror and fear that he is already feeling, for the second time.

Along with this ringing, and because he has hidden in a room freshly painted, Raskolnikov will later be plagued by the smell of fresh paint. For example, when his landlady has him summoned to the police office, the smell of fresh paint there contributes to his fainting spell.

Part One ends with the murder and Raskolnikov's illness. The crime occupies only one part of the book; the remainder of the novel will deal with the punishment.

Part Two
Chapter 1

Summary

After the murder, Raskolnikov collapses into a deep sleep. Upon awakening, he is terrified; he has slept for so long that he fears that he is going mad. He remembers the items that he had stolen and his failure to hide them or to lock the door of his flat—this was madness. As he hides the items, he begins to wonder if his punishment is already beginning and after a few stirrings and attempts to hide his loot in a hole in his room, he surrendered himself to mingled sleep and delirium.

Again he awakens to Nastasya's pounding. The porter is with her and he hands Raskolnikov a summons to report to the police. Nastasya does not want him to move since he has had a fever since the day before. As he dresses, he is repulsed by the thought of wearing the bloody socks, but since he has no others, he is forced to do so. On the way to the police station, he thinks that he might just confess it all and be done with it: "I shall go in, fall on my knees, and tell the whole story."

When he reaches the police station, he is almost overwhelmed by the "sickening smell of fresh paint. . .from the newly decorated rooms." The small crowded rooms, the lack of fresh air, the confusion as to why he is there, and the intolerable waiting make him feverish. Finally, he discovers that his landlady is suing him for back rent. As Raskolnikov is told of his offense, he goes into a rather lengthy explanation of his relationship to his landlady and of his previous engagement to his landlady's daughter. The police instruct him to sign an I.O.U. and release him. As he signs the paper, he overhears the police discussing the murder of Alyona Ivanovna and Lizaveta, and he faints. When he recovers, he hurries home thinking that the police suspect him of the murder.

Commentary

In a novel with six parts and an epilogue, one can easily argue that the first part is a prologue because only that part is devoted to the crime and the remaining parts are devoted to the punishment that begins immediately with his hatred of the blood on his clothes and especially on his socks, and the loss of his ability to retain complete control over all of his faculties.

Crime therefore is a demanding, troublesome matter that becomes a colossal nuisance. And crime is accompanied by various types of illnesses—with Raskolnikov, it is expressed in his temperature, his inability to function normally, and his dread of the very blood that he has just shed. When it is necessary to put on the bloody socks, his repulsion indicates his dread of or living with his murder. This scene contrasts well with the later scene when he is splattered with blood from the death of Marmeladov. In this later scene, he had no qualms about touching blood *per se*.

When he receives the police summons, his mind is in such a state of agitation that he forgets that Nastasya had told him earlier that his landlady was going to have him summoned.

As he approaches the police station, he thinks of confessing for the third time. At the police station, he needs to confess something; therefore, he tells of the most intimate event in his past life, that is, the engagement to his landlady's daughter. He even confesses that she was not attractive. This is the fourth time he considers confession, and his engagement to the landlady's daughter shows his empathy with suffering humanity. Shortly after this his fifth thought of confession follows when he thinks that he should confess everything: "to get up at once, to go up to Nikodim Fomitch, and tell him everything." The tenseness and fear of being summoned to the police station for the murder prompt these thoughts of confession.

At the end of the chapter, Raskolnikov's fainting spell is a result of the tension caused by the summons; the oppressive smell of the new paint, which reminds him of the murder scene; the crowded conditions with its lack of fresh air; and finally the discussion of the murder of Alyona Ivanovna. This fainting spell will later become a cause of suspicion and will be used by Porfiry.

Part Two
Chapter 2

Summary

Upon leaving the police station, Raskolnikov is afraid that the police have searched his room, but he soon sees that no one has entered his room. He empties all of his "loot" into his pockets and plans to hide it somewhere. After walking a long way, he finds himself in a park. He moves a huge rock aside and hides his stolen goods under the rock.

He remembers that he had promised himself that he would visit his friend Razumihkin the day after the murder and he goes to his room. Raskolnikov says that he has come to ask for lessons, but after a while he suddenly changes his mind and leaves amid Razumihkin's entreaties to know where he is going and where he is living. Raskolnikov ignores him and leaves.

Raskolnikov walks absent-mindedly toward the river and is almost run down by a coach and is actually struck with a whip by a coachman. As he stands rubbing his back, he suddenly feels someone thrust money into his hand because he looked so much like a beggar. He immediately throws the money away.

When he returns home, he dreams that the police officer Ilya Petrovitch is beating his landlady. He is awakened by Nastasya who realizes that he is sick and who goes to get him some water just as he collapses into unconsciousness.

Commentary

At the beginning of the chapter, Raskolnikov is determined to get rid of all of Alyona's things. At first he wants to throw them into the canal so all traces would be gone, but then he walks through the park and hides them safely under a large stone. During all this activity, he never bothered to examine the items in order to determine their value.

This failure to count his theft suggests that the murder was not committed either for need of money or for the purpose of helping mankind by using the money.

Earlier, he had maintained that he would go to Razumihkin's after he had committed the crime. This act of murder, if he can ignore it, would therefore make him a superior (extraordinary) person. But he is also in need of human contact. We later find out that part of Raskolnikov's theory about crime is that it isolates one from human contact. But once he arrives at Razumihkin's, he recognizes this need for society to be a weakness, that the Ubermensch must be able to stand completely alone. He must be above and beyond wanting, needing, or receiving any sympathy or help. It was a weakness on his part to go, and, as he recognizes this weakness, he immediately leaves Razumihkin's room. This same view will also separate him from his mother and sister because the Ubermensch must be able to stand alone and shun human contact, especially human sympathy.

The pathetic and confused state of Raskolnikov's condition is illustrated by his stumbling in front of a coach and being struck with a lash and then being mistaken for a beggar. This beating and the subsequent charity function as ironic contrasts to Raskolnikov's theory. It shows him to be one of the weak who are subjected to these indignities rather than being one of the extraordinary men who are above the need of help.

Glossary

"You are smoking a cigarette" In nineteenth-century Russia it was considered rude, offensive, and disrespectful to smoke indoors in the presence of others and totally taboo for women to smoke in public.

Herr Kapitan This is German for Mr. Captain.

Voznesensky Prospect This is the street that leads into a courtyard surrounded by four blank walls where Raskolnikov lifts up a large stone, buries his loot, and replaces the stone.

Part Two
Chapter 3

Summary

Raskolnikov remains in a limbo between consciousness and delirium for several days during which Nastasya and Razumihkin take care of him. When he awakens, he discovers a stranger in his room. The stranger has come to deposit with him 35 rubles that his mother has sent to him. Raskolnikov tries to refuse the money, but Razumihkin insists that he take it and still protesting, he signs an acknowledgment of the receipt of the money.

Razumihkin chides Raskolnikov because he has been so detached and distant from his landlady, who is after all, very shy and very nice. Razumihkin reveals that he has been able to cajole the landlady into being of great service to them. He tells also of the good attention by Dr. Zossimov who has been in constant attendance to him. He tells how Zametov, the police chief, has also visited him, and when Raskolnikov is upset, Razumihkin explains that Zametov only wanted to get to know him. He also tells how Raskolnikov has been almost neurotic about clutching his dirty socks while he was unconscious. Raskolnikov is bewildered by all of the attention being paid to him.

As Raskolnikov goes back to sleep, Razumihkin takes some of the money and goes out to buy new clothes for Raskolnikov, and with the help of Nastasya, they put his new clothes on him.

Commentary

Raskolnikov's illness supports his own theory in which he states that either illness or disease give rise to crime or crime is always accompanied by something akin to disease. Raskolnikov's state of illness, his psychotic desire to hold his bloody socks, his fever, and his delirium indicate the beginnings of his punishment.

Raskolnikov's attempt to reject the money again expresses his view that the Ubermensch (or extraordinary man or superior man) should not be obligated to anyone; he must be absolutely independent of everyone.

Zametov's visit and interest in Raskolnikov has absolutely nothing to do with his crime—instead, he is concerned about the complaints and summons that Raskolnikov's landlady has registered against him. The easy and affectionate way in which Razumihkin is able to handle Raskolnikov's landlady again emphasizes Raskolnikov's isolation and abnormality because of his failure to see with what ease he could have controlled her, thus obviating the summons from the police—a summons that ironically is served concurrent with the crime.

The recovery from the illness and the new clothes symbolically suggest that Raskolnikov will now begin his path towards recovery, redemption, and salvation.

Glossary

Rousseau Jean-Jacques Rousseau wrote in his famous *Confessions (1781-88)* "Myself, myself alone; I might not be better, but at least I am different." It is ironic that at the time Raskolnikov is thinking how his theories have set him apart from other men, he would be translating Rousseau.

Radischev Alexander Radischev was a leading liberal Russian writer who attacked the abuses of the serfdom system and also the judicial system, which allowed men to own other men—that is, serfdom. Raskolnikov considered himself to be aligned with these forward-thinking people.

thirty-five roubles The amount of money that Raskolnikov's mother sent him would have been $17.50. It is not a small sum when one considers the spending value at that time.

clothes from Scharmer This was the name of a famous store featuring Western style clothing. Dostoevsky bought all of his clothing there.

Part Two
Chapter 4

Summary

Dr. Zossimov appears to check up on his patient's progress. Razumihkin is eager to know if Raskolnikov can attend a function he is having that night for his old uncle from the provinces. Also Zametov, the chief clerk, will be there along with Porfiry Petrovitch, the examining magistrate and "a graduate of the College of Jurisprudence."

As Zossimov and Razumihkin talk of the arrest of two painters for the murder of Alyona and Lizaveta Ivanovna, unlike his usual lethargic self, Raskolnikov is intensely interested in this discussion. Razumihkin is very firm in his stand that the painters could not have committed the crime and makes an elaborate defense of their innocence. Zossimov notices that the discussion excites Raskolnikov and thinks that this interest in the crime suggests that he is regaining an interest in life.

Commentary

This chapter introduces the character of Porfiry Petrovitch, who will become Raskolnikov's adversary and actually his friend even though Raskolnikov will not admit the latter.

The essence of the chapter is Razumihkin and Zossimov's discussion of the murder and the arrest of the house painters for the murder. The entire discussion excites Raskolnikov so much that Zossimov thinks that he is almost recovered from his illness. Razumihkin's strong defense of the painters becomes ironic when later, in Part Four, Nikolai, one of the painters, confesses to the crime (albeit a false confession).

The long and difficult explanation of the crime—a discussion that involves many new names and theories of guilt that later prove false—must be viewed as some sort of filler for the newspaper in which the novel was being serialized.

Part Two
Chapter 5

Summary

Dunya's fiancé arrives at Raskolnikov's room dressed to the hilt ("starchy and pompous") and introduces himself as though everyone already knows who he is. As Luzhin makes feeble and awkward attempts to explain who he is, Raskolnikov remains sullen and silent. When Luzhin tells of the living accommodations he has made for Dunya and Pulcheria Alexandrovna, everyone immediately recognizes the apartment as "a disgusting place—filthy, stinking, and what's more, of doubtful character." Luzhin excuses this because he is also new in town and does not know his way around. Then, when Luzhin tells that he is living with Lebezyatnikov, a name that Raskolnikov had heard from Marmeladov in an unfavorable light, the trend of the conversation returns to the murder.

Razumihkin announces that the police are "examining all who have left pledges with her [Alyona]." As soon as the conversation can be turned to Luzhin's engagement, Raskolnikov accuses him of trying only to make Dunya feel indebted to him. Luzhin protests that Raskolnikov's mother has misrepresented him. At this point, Raskolnikov threatens to "send him flying downstairs" if he ever mentions his mother again and orders him to "go to hell." As Zossimov and Razumihkin notice this sudden outburst, they also notice that Raskolnikov takes an immense interest in the murder.

Commentary

The arrival of Luzhin is not propitious at this time. First, it is the end of Raskolnikov's illness; second, it interrupts the discussion about the murders; third, Raskolnikov has already developed a dislike for him from his mother's letters; fourth, Luzhin arrives at Raskolnikov's cramped and small quarters dressed in clothes too new, too formal, too pompous, and his behavior is snobbish, patronizing, and condescending. And then, fifth, when he tells of the living quarters he has obtained for his fiancée and her mother, he reveals himself as a cheap, penny-pinching miser. According to Razumihkin, the hotel is "a horrible place, dirty and stinking, and its character is suspect." Our future exposure to Luzhin reveals that Raskolnikov is entirely correct in his violent dislike for the man, who will later stoop to utter villainy in accusing Sonya of stealing from him and trying to frame her and disgrace her.

Raskolnikov also learns that Porfiry is examining all of those whose pledges were left with Alyona Ivanovna. If he had thought everything out before murdering the pawnbroker, he would have taken time to search out and destroy his own pledge, affirming once again that Raskolnikov committed murder before he had "all of the details worked out." He also realizes that he must take the initiative and go himself to confront Porfiry, his perceived antagonist.

Glossary

Luzhin's ideas Generally speaking, the reader should be aware that Luzhin's ideas are all a paraphrase and an oversimplification of known writers of the time. Most of these ideas come from a novel by N.B. Chernyshevsky, *What Is to Be Done?* (or sometimes translated *What Should Be Done?*). Essentially, Dostoevsky rejected most of the ideas expressed in this novel and, therefore, having Luzhkin repeat these objectionable ideas makes Luzhkin look the more foolish and increases Raskolnikov's dislike of the person.

Part Two
Chapter 6

Summary

Alone, Raskolnikov immediately dresses in his new clothes, takes all the money that is left over from the purchase of his new clothes, and escapes from his room. He walks towards the Hay Market, where he encounters a 15 year old to whom he gives five kopecks. He is furthermore drawn toward a saloon in search of human fellowship. He then remembers the horror of being confined to living on a square yard of space all his life: "only to live, to live no matter how—only to live." He then resolves to live life whatever it may be.

He leaves the saloon and enters a clean restaurant where he asks for the newspapers of the last five days, beginning with the day of the murder and followed by the days of his illness. While he is reading the papers, he meets Zametov, the minor official in the police department and a friend to Razumihkin.

As the two begin a conversation, Raskolnikov begins to taunt Zametov telling him about his activities and motivations. He tells him that he came to the restaurant solely for the purpose of reading about the murder of the old pawnbroker. In fact, he confesses his extreme concern about the entire episode. When Zametov explains how the police are all wrong in the manner they are conducting the case, Raskolnikov begins to resent the implication that the crime was obviously performed by an amateur. As a result of this resentment, he offers what he thinks would be a perfect way of committing the crime and how one should go about hiding the money and the jewels. Raskolnikov's explanations and suggestion that he might be the one who murdered the old pawnbroker and her half sister disturbs Zametov who dismisses it as an aftermath to Raskolnikov's illness.

Outside, he runs into Razumihkin and he tells him of his annoyance at being followed. "I don't want your kindness. . .I may be ungrateful, perhaps I am mean and base, only leave me alone, all of you, for

God's sake leave me alone!! Leave me alone!" Razumihkin is so shocked at this outburst that he allows Raskolnikov to go his own way and immediately realizes that the outburst is part of Raskolnikov's illness.

After Raskolnikov has escaped, he goes to a bridge where he is a witness to a woman's attempt to drown herself. He realizes that he was going to attempt the same thing and then becomes disgusted with himself for even thinking about it. He then returns to the scene of the crime. He is amazed to find the entire apartment being repainted. It no longer looks the same as when he was last in it. He then goes to the doorbell and begins to ring it, listening and remembering the "hideous and agonizingly fearful sensation he has felt when he was trapped after the crime." When the painters demand to know what he is doing there, he tells them to come with him to the police station and he will tell everything. At the end of the chapter, he is fully resolved to go to the police himself and confess everything.

Commentary

Character Insight

As noted earlier, by dressing in his new clothes and accepting the money from his mother, Raskolnikov is ready to move in the direction of redemption. On his walk, his first act is to give five kopecks to a 15-year-old street singer, an act of human compassion. In another incident, he gave a wench begging for 6 kopecks a total of 15 kopecks. Feeling his own compassion, his thoughts turn to living even if he is "confined to a square yard of space it is better than immediate death"— a thought that becomes a motif which he rejects or accepts according to his desire to live.

When he enters a cafe to have tea, he asks for the newspapers of the last five or six days. Throughout Europe, cafes always have newspapers and often the latest magazines for their customers to read, and Raskolnikov takes advantage of this custom to request the papers of the last five or six days when he was anti-social and then ill. Here in the cafe, he meets Zametov and thinks of confession for the sixth time. This time, however it is a type of real confession: "Now I will declare to you. . .no, better, I'll confess," but the way the confession is made makes Zametov see it only as a result of Raskolnikov's delirium and sickness. His explanation follows exactly the same steps that he had taken himself in committing the crime. At the end of the explanation, Raskolnikov asks "And what if it was I who murdered the old woman and Lizaveta?"

The confession, however, is not as readily dismissed by Zametov as Raskolnikov believes, and later it is used as part of Zametov's suspicion against Raskolnikov.

Raskolnikov is offended when Zametov suggests that the murderer was inexperienced and rather inept. And to prove to himself that Zametov is wrong, Raskolnikov presents the exact description of how he hid the stolen property. Even though Raskolnikov is horrified at his own murder, he is still resentful that others would find fault with it.

Theme

When he meets Razumihkin again, he becomes adamant that he should be left alone, we have the manifestations of the Ubermensch who feels that he must act alone in order to establish his superiority.

When Raskolnikov goes to the bridge with the apparent intent to commit suicide, he first observes the unknown woman's attempt to drown herself and he reminds himself again of existing on "the square yard of space" and again there is the seventh thought of confession, which is motivated this time by the nearness of the suicide.

Raskolnikov's return to the scene of the crime supports the theory that crime is partly a disease since it is a neurotic desire that draws him back to the murder scene. When questioned by the painters, he offers to take them to the police station and confess all to them—the eighth time that he contemplates confession. Then standing at the crossroads, for the ninth time, he contemplates confession. This time he resolves to go in order to end the torment of doubt as to whether he is an Ubermensch.

Glossary

"Tea and old newspapers appeared" In Russia as well as most European nations, a person went into a coffee or tea house to drink and, more importantly, to read the papers that were kept by the establishment.

pood A Russian unit of weight, equal to 36.11 pounds.

Voznesensky Bridge This is the bridge where Raskolnikov witnesses a woman attempting suicide just as he has been contemplating suicide himself.

Part Two
Chapter 7

Summary

On his way to the police station, Raskolnikov witnesses a terrible accident—a drunken man stumbles and falls under a carriage and is crushed. Amid great confusion, Raskolnikov recognizes the wounded man as Marmeladov, and he immediately takes charge and offers money to anyone who will help get him home.

When they arrive, Katerina Ivanovna becomes hysterical and cannot control her grief and anxiety—the children are hungry, they have no money for a burial, and she has no one to turn to. Raskolnikov offers consolation and again offers to pay for a doctor and other expenses. A priest is sent for, and Katerina Ivanovna also sends young Polenka to tell Sonya.

When the doctor arrives, he announces that Marmeladov will die immediately. He receives the funeral rites, and Polenka returns saying that Sonya is coming immediately. Marmeladov tries to make some apology to Katerina and to Sonya who has just arrived, dressed in the gaudy, cheap finery worn by prostitutes: "She seemed forgetful of her garish fourth-hand silk dress, indecently out of place here with its ridiculous long train and immense crinoline."

When Raskolnikov first sees Sonya, he "recognized her crushed and ashamed in her humiliation. . .meekly awaiting her turn to say goodby to her dying father." The father had never seen his daughter in her professional costume; infinite shame possessed both father and daughter.

As Raskolnikov leaves, he gives his money to Katerina Ivanovna and outside he meets Nikodim Fomitch, the police official who exclaims that Raskolnikov is splattered with blood. At Sonya's request, Polenka follows Raskolnikov to find out his name, where he lives, and to thank him. In their meeting, Raskolnikov shows great compassion for young

Polenka and asks her to pray for him. He then resolves that life is still before him and he rejects any thoughts of confessing to his crime. With this thought, he goes to Razumihkin and apologizes for his bad temper. Razumihkin walks home with him and tells him of Zossimov's suspicion that perhaps Raskolnikov is going insane. When they reach Raskolnikov's place, they find his mother and sister waiting for him. Instead of returning their enthusiastic embraces, he faints.

Commentary

At the end of Chapter 6, Raskolnikov was determined to go to the police and confess. On the way, when he witnesses the death of a human being run over by a carriage, he is automatically reminded of the previous episode when he was hit by a carriage and brutally treated. Therefore, his indignation causes him to respond to the wounded man, who turns out to be Marmeladov. In this incident, his intellectual desire to confess is overruled by his emotional and humanitarian responses. His intellectual side is always deliberate while his emotional responses are spontaneous.

Theme

In Marmeladov's apartment, the reader is exposed to the cry of "Do you know what it means to have no place to go." Raskolnikov is therefore affected by the poverty and squalor of the place and constantly volunteers to pay for any expenses. At the end, Raskolnikov's compassion causes him to give his last 20 rubles to Katerina to help. This is the money that he has just received from his mother—money that she could hardly spare and not for him to squander on some poor family. Again, even though Raskolnikov can rationalize a murder, he cannot stand the sight of human suffering, indicating the tremendous poles of his existence.

Character Insight

Raskolnikov's first sight of Sonya reveals her as a person of great suffering and shame. He will later say that Sonya represents the great sufferings of all humanity. Here he is equally aware of the contrast between the absurd finery and gaudy dress required by prostitution as seen against her demure and humiliated self. He is immediately attracted to her, not for sexual reasons, but because of her great suffering.

Physically, Raskolnikov is an exceptionally handsome man, and now Dostoevsky presents Sonya as small, but very pretty with lovely hair and remarkable blue eyes.

While helping with Marmeladov, Raskolnikov becomes splattered with blood. Whereas Alyona's blood on his person after the murder was a part of the cause of his delirium and was repulsive to him, this blood from helping Marmeladov makes him determined again to live. When he tells the police magistrate, Nikodim Fomitch, "I am all over covered with blood" he means this both literally (from helping Marmeladov) and figuratively (from killing Alyona) and he decides to live. And his meeting with young Polenka also influences him to live. "Life is real! haven't I lived just now? My life has not yet died with that old woman!" But with his affirmation of life, he renews his acquaintance with Razumihkin, so as to have an excuse for going personally to Porfiry rather than to the police station.

Part II ends with the surprise appearance of his mother and sister, and the emotions are too much for him and he faints.

Glossary

"Ach, mein Gott!" "Oh my God!" Dostoevsky uses both the German phrase and a humorous type of German speech pattern for the purpose of satirizing the landlady and satirizing Germans in general.

Sonya's dress When Sonya appears, she is dressed in a dress of her profession. A prostitute dressed in gaudy finery identifies her profession, thus she looks out of place in this outfit.

Part Three
Chapter 1

Summary

After Raskolnikov recovers from his fainting spell, everyone seems at a loss for something to say. Without warning, Raskolnikov throws a dark cloud over everything by announcing that he is not only violently opposed to Dunya's engagement, but he also forbids her to sacrifice herself to such a scoundrel as Luzhin. He says "I may be infamous, and even so, I would disown such a sister."

Razumihkin attributes Raskolnikov's outburst to his illness and suggests that it would be better to leave him alone for the present. When Pulcheria Alexandrovna wants to remain with her son, Razumihkin points out that Dunya cannot remain alone in such dreadful lodgings that Luzhin has secured for them. When all agree, he escorts them to their lodgings, promising to return later and bring Dr. Zossimov with him. Razumihkin, is so enthralled with Dunya that at one point, he gets down on his knees in the middle of the street and kisses her hand. He has obviously formed a sudden and strong infatuation for Dunya.

Commentary

Raskolnikov's bizarre behavior is alarming to his mother, which allows the drunken Razumihkin to take charge. In this meeting, Dostoevsky is establishing a relationship between Dunya and Razumihkin so that when Raskolnikov finally confesses his guilt, it will leave him free from practical worries about his family so that he can concentrate upon his own actions and guilt.

Thus far the reader has been constantly with Raskolnikov and has seen everything from his point of view; now suddenly, he is left alone and the point of view shifts to Razumihkin and his relationship with Raskolnikov's family. Even though his actions are in a "drunken excess," both Pulcheria and Dunya are drawn to this good person.

Part Three
Chapter 2

Summary

Razumihkin awakens the next day remembering everything about his talk the preceding night and he is ashamed. He now washes and dresses in clean clothes before reporting to Dunya and Pulcheria Alexandrovna. He goes to check with Dr. Zossimov who is satisfied with Raskolnikov's progress but is disturbed about his monomania concerning the painters and the murders.

Razumihkin goes immediately to Pulcheria Alexandrovna who wants to hear about her son. He tells that he has known Rodya for almost two years and that at times Rodya fluctuates between two characters. "He has been suspicious and fanciful. He has a noble nature and a kind heart. He does not like showing his feelings and he is not at all morbid, but simply cold and inhumanly callous. Really it is as though he had two separate personalities," and he fluctuates between two aspects of his character. Razumihkin then tells of Raskolnikov's past engagement to the landlady's daughter who was an invalid, queer, and positively plain if not ugly.

Pulcheria, with Dunya's permission, shows Razumihkin a letter received this morning from Luzhin. In it he writes of his involvement until tomorrow night when he will call on them. He explicitly, earnestly, and "imperatively request the Rodion Romanovitch shall not be present at our meeting." He further threatens that if his request is ignored, he shall leave. He then reports that he has seen Raskolnikov in the flat of a notorious drunk who was run over and dying, and "he gave the daughter, a notoriously ill-conducted female [that is, a prostitute] almost twenty-five roubles."

Pulcheria Alexandrovna cannot understand her son's actions as reported by Luzhin. They leave to go see Raskolnikov, but Pulcheria Alexandrovna is so frightened to see her son that she can hardly stand up.

Commentary

This chapter shows Razumihkin's intense feelings for Dunya and helps prepare the way for him to take over caring for the family while Raskolnikov is involved with his guilt. The long description of Raskolnikov emphasizes his split personality and describes his dual personality "as though he were alternating between two characters." In using such terms as "split personality," one is using a term that has not yet been coined by Sigmund Freud, but Dostoevsky was fully aware of the quirks of one's personality even though they had no label.

Character Insight

The mention of Raskolnikov's desire to marry the ugly, queer, invalid daughter of his landlady illustrates Raskolnikov's predilection for the weak and the downtrodden and helps to explain his later attraction to Sonya.

Luzhin's attempt to cause dissension between Raskolnikov and his mother by suggesting that Raskolnikov gave money to Sonya, a prostitute, rather than to Katerina Ivanovna, shows what a despicable character he is and how right Raskolnikov was to see this petty, ugly side of Dunya's fiancé. His request that Raskolnikov not be present at their interview is another attempt to alienate Raskolnikov from his family, thus making them more dependent on Luzhin.

The reader should further note that after being constantly with Raskolnikov, it is unusual that we have an entire chapter without his presence. It is necessary, however, so that the relationship between Razumihkin and Dunya can progress, and also prepares us for Raskolnikov's dependence on Sonya.

Glossary

maestro The word means master in Italian and refers basically to a master of music.

a Rubinstein A Russian concert pianist (Anton Rubinstein, 1829-94) whose name lends itself to anyone who plays the piano exceptionally well.

Part Three
Chapter 3

Summary

Dr. Zossimov reports that Raskolnikov is much better, but he is still pale, abstracted, and gloomy and looks "like a man who has been wounded or suffered intense pain." He concludes that whatever caused this collapse, they must remove these unhealthy influences.

Pulcheria Alexandrovna is so pleased to see her son that she narrates with deep emotion their fear upon arriving in St. Petersburg since Luzhin was unable to meet them. They were frightened to be alone, and she asks her son if he knows what it is like to be utterly alone. Raskolnikov then remembers Marmeladov's aloneness and tells that he has given all of the money she sent him to a poor woman whose husband was just killed. He admits that it was not right of him—that to help others a man must have the right to do so—and he had no right to squander his mother's hard-to-come-by money.

Raskolnikov then begins to feel impatient with his mother, even though he remembers how much he loves them in their absence. Pulcheria suddenly announces that Marfa Petrovna was dead and attributes it to her husband's beating her. Suddenly, Raskolnikov cannot stand their presence and "makes for the door" but is detained. Raskolnikov tells of his affair with the landlady's daughter and describes how plain she was, but even if she had been lame "or hump-backed" he "might have loved her even more." He insists that Dunya cannot marry Luzhin: "I do not withdraw from my chief point. It is me or Luzhin. If I am a scoundrel, you must not be. One is enough. If you marry Luzhin, I cease at once to look on you as a sister."

Dunya makes an elaborate justification of her engagement and then suddenly, with no provocation or reason, Raskolnikov withdraws his objections saying "Marry whom you like!" Dunya shows him Luzhin's letter, and Raskolnikov, amused by it, simply comments that Luzhin wants "to slander me and to raise dissension between us." Dunya implores Raskolnikov to come to the interview. She also invites Razumihkin.

Commentary

Theme

Pulcheria asks her son if he knows what "it is like to be utterly alone?"; this question is the recurring motif introduced first by Marmeladov, then picked up by Raskolnikov and applied to Sonya and to himself. The effect of this utterance on Raskolnikov is profound since he has just recovered from the same emotions and the same desperation.

Raskolnikov has the sudden realization that the crime, rather than making him above the ordinary man, imprisons him and isolates him from others, even his mother: "It became suddenly plain and perceptible that he would never again be able to speak freely of anything to anyone."

Character Insight

Raskolnikov's dual personality is emphasized again and again in the chapter. At one moment he renews his objections to Dunya's marriage to Luzhin: "If you marry Luzhin, I cease to look on you as a sister." This is his compassionate, humane side speaking now in which he sees his sister sacrificing herself by entering into an insufferable marriage. Then only a few seconds later, he suddenly reverses: "What am I making such a fuss a for? Marry whom you like." Of course, this particular reversal from compassionate to intellectual is brought about by Dunya's terrible justification of her marriage. "If I ruin anyone, it is only myself. I am not committing a murder." This statement forces Raskolnikov to realize that he committed his murder so as to see if he would be able to stand apart and above other human beings; therefore, he must assume this air of not caring whom Dunya marries.

Ultimately, the question of whether to invite Raskolnikov to the meeting with Luzhin must occur before Dunya has knowledge of the money left to her by Marfa Petrovna so that her risking her marriage with Luzhin does not involve money matters. She proves herself to be a true agent and later worthy of the love of Razumihkin.

Part Three
Chapter 4

Summary

The family conference is suddenly interrupted by the appearance of Sonya, dressed in modest simplicity, filled with embarrassment and humility. She has come at Katerina Ivanovna's insistence to entreat Rodya to be present at the funeral and refreshments afterwards. He offers her a seat and tells her he needs to speak with her. She is further embarrassed because she should not be sitting in the presence of Dunya and Pulcheria Alexandrovna. She is also in Rodya's "bedroom" and she realizes that due to the poverty of his room that Raskolnikov must have given them everything.

Dunya and her mother must leave and alone, the mother has a presentiment that there is a special meaning of some importance between Rodya and Sonya, particularly after what Luzhin had written about her. Dunya decides that Luzhin is "a wretched scandal-monger."

Raskolnikov wants to be alone with Sonya, but first he tells Razumihkin that he needs to arrange an interview with Porfiry. Sonya has to go, and as she leaves, she is followed by Svidrigailov who discovers that they live in adjoining rooms.

As Raskolnikov and Razumihkin are on their was to see Porfiry, Raskolnikov begins teasing Razumihkin of being in love with Dunya and of acting like a love-sick Romeo. Rodya points out that Razumihkin has shaved and bathed, put on "clean linen," and has "Pomatum" on his hair. They enter Porfiry Petrovitch's flat laughing loudly.

Commentary

This chapter is the most disjointed (or the least unified) of any chapter. First there is the group in Raskolnikov's small room. Secondly, we shift to a street conversation between Dunya and her mother. Thirdly, a discussion outside with Rodya, Sonya, and Razumihkin, and fourth, Sonya leaves and is trailed by Svidrigailov, and finally, a scene between Rodya and Razumihkin where Rodya teases him about being a Romeo. This rambling chapter is not at all typical of the rest of the novel.

During the time of this novel, Sonya's appearance at Raskolnikov's is a social error and for him to have her sit with his mother and sister is a tremendous breach of social class and can be construed as a deep insult to mother and sister. Raskolnikov's terrible error can be explained in that he instinctively or subconsciously knows that Sonya will become his means of salvation.

The scene with Sonya's returning to her home introduces the very important personage of Svidrigailov. Our first impression is that he is secretively trailing her for dubious reasons. He does live next door to Sonya, and this nearness allows him the chance to overhear Rodya's confession to Sonya.

The chapter ends with Raskolnikov's deliberate joviality as they approach Porfiry apartment so as to deceive Porfiry, making him think all is light-hearted and healthy. This event shows the return of Raskolnikov's calm, rational powers.

Glossary

monomaniac Someone who is overwhelmingly possessed by one single idea, such as Ahab's obsession about the white whale in *Moby Dick*. Raskolnikov's obsession with the murder and blood rouses suspicions in Porfiry during the investigations.

"Crevez, chiens, si vous n'etes pas contents" "Die, dogs, if you are content [happy]." [French]

"Good-bye Rodya, or rather au revoir" Razumihkin does not like the Russian word for "good-bye," which has an air of finality to it; instead he substitutes the French "au revoir," which means simply "till we see each other again."

Part Three
Chapter 5

Summary

Raskolnikov enters Porfiry's place trying to conceal his laughter. He is surprised to see Zametov, the chief clerk of the police department. He is then introduced to Porfiry. He tells his host of his official business: He had left Alyona Ivanovna some small items not of much value, to which he attached great sentimental value, particularly a watch left him by his father. Porfiry announced that he had indeed been expecting Raskolnikov, since everyone else who had pledges with the old pawnbroker had already made their claims.

Porfiry lets Raskolnikov know that he knew all about his pledges and they had been wrapped up carefully by the old pawnbroker and dated with his name on them. Porfiry subtly lets Raskolnikov know that he is aware of Raskolnikov's sickness, of his meeting with Zametov, and of his presence at Marmeladov's death. All these revelations disturb him, and he thinks to himself that Porfiry is playing with him, "like a cat plays with a mouse." He momentarily thinks of confessing the whole truth, especially since he feels that the police already know everything.

A discussion of the relationship of crime to one's environment ensues, which leads to Porfiry's announcement that he has read Raskolnikov's article on crime, which had appeared in a prominent magazine two months ago. Everyone, including Raskolnikov, is surprised that the article has indeed been published. Porfiry then asks Raskolnikov to explain parts of his theory in more detail, which he undertakes to do.

The essence of Raskolnikov's theory about crime as he presents it involves the duties and obligations of a class of people classified as the "ordinary people" as contrasted to the "extraordinary people." He outlines that (1) the perpetration of a crime is always accompanied by illness. Either the illness causes a person to commit the crime or else committing the crime causes one to become ill. (2) All men are divided into "ordinary" and "extraordinary." (3) Ordinary men have to live in submission and have no right to transgress the law because they are ordinary. (4) On the contrary, the extraordinary man has the right to commit any crime and to transgress the law in any way because he is extraordinary. That is not an official legal right but an inner right to decide in his own conscience whether to overstep the law or any obstacle that stands in the way of the practical fulfillment of his idea. (5) All great men would (or should) have the right to eliminate a few men in order to make their discoveries known to the benefit of all humanity. (6) All great men capable of giving something new (some "New Word") must not submit to the common law, or if they do, then this is proof that they do not belong among the extraordinary people. Being great means breaking from the common rut of ordinary laws. (7) In conclusion, men are divided into two categories the inferior (or ordinary) who can only reproduce their kind, and the superior "men who have the gift or talent to utter a new word."

After his explanation, Porfiry subtly wonders if Raskolnikov might have thought of himself as being "extraordinary" while composing or formulating this particular theory. Raskolnikov maintains that even if he did think that, he would not tell Porfiry, but he assures him that he does not consider himself to be a Napoleon or a Mahomet. Porfiry wonders then if this superior person would suffer, and Raskolnikov responds that "suffering and pain are always obligatory on those of wide intellect and profound feeling."

After hearing the explanation, Porfiry then returns to the business of the pledges and asks Raskolnikov if he remembers seeing some painters at work there. Raskolnikov feels that there is a trap here somewhere and tells that he cannot recall seeing any painters, but that someone was moving out. Razumihkin reminds Porfiry that the painters were only at work on the day of the murder and that Raskolnikov's last time there was several days before the murder. Porfiry pretends to have been confused and offers Raskolnikov his apologies.

Commentary

This chapter presents us a full view of the 35-year-old Porfiry, and it is immediately apparent that Raskolnikov has a worthy opponent. For example, in the discussion of Raskolnikov's article on crime, Porfiry wants to know if while he was composing it Raskolnikov didn't consider himself to be an extraordinary person because he has uttered a new word. That is, if Raskolnikov's theory is believed, then he must have considered himself extraordinary, even though he assures Porfiry that he is no Napoleon or Mahomet.

Even though Raskolnikov disclaims his pretensions to being an extraordinary man, nevertheless, what is new, really new and original in his theory (thus possibly making him one of the extraordinary) is that he "sanctions bloodshed in the name of conscience." That is, the great man is obligated to give to the world his new word, and if it means killing a person (or a louse) in order to do so, then the great man must do that.

Porfiry is also very clever when he asks Raskolnikov in a casual, off-handed manner if he by chance saw two painters when he went to the pawnbroker's. This is a trap, and Raskolnikov knows it is because there were no painters on the day he pawned his watch, but there were painters there on the day Alyona was murdered. Raskolnikov is clever enough to discover the trap and thus escape. His perception of this trap again shows the return of his rational powers. Consequently, Porfiry is, as Raskolnikov earlier thought, playing "cat and mouse" games with him.

Theme

If there seem to be contradictions in parts of Raskolnikov's theory, such as maintaining that the great will suffer and also later that the great must be above sympathy and dependence on the ordinary, these contradictions are not unintentional on Dostoevsky's part. Instead, it must be emphasized that Raskolnikov at the time of the murder had not worked out his theory in complete detail. The contradictions exist so that later Raskolnikov will have to justify them when he is trying to explain his crime to Sonya.

Part Three
Chapter 6

Summary

Raskolnikov and Razumihkin leave Porfiry's to meet with Dunya and Pulcheria; they discuss the implications of the conversation about the murder, and Raskolnikov is certain that he is suspected. Razumihkin is infuriated that suspicion is cast upon Rodya, and he plans to reprimand his distant relative, Porfiry.

Just as they reach the rooming house where his mother and sister are staying, Rodya parts from Razumihkin promising to return shortly. The parting is again difficult. Rodya flees to his room to search for any scraps of evidence, but he can find nothing.

As he is leaving his room, the porter points out a man who was inquiring after him. When approached, the mysterious stranger calls him "Murderer!" and leaves. Even though Rodya follows him, nothing is resolved. This episode leaves him visibly agitated and confused, and rather than going to his mother's, he returns to his room and sleeps.

Alone, he begins to examine the basis of his theory. He still believes in the nobility of the theory, but he worries about whether he might not have destroyed some of its nobility by practicing it on a disgusting object like the old pawnbroker. Napoleon was a real ruler "to whom everything is permitted," but he cannot believe Napoleon, who conquered "the pyramids" and "destroyed Toulon," would ever "crawl under a vile old woman's bed." He then realizes that he "killed not a human being but a principle." Furthermore, he feels that he may also be a louse, and he again thinks of confession.

He falls asleep and dreams that he is again striking the old pawnbroker, but this time she refuses to die. When he awakens from this dreadful dream, he notices Svidrigailov standing in his doorway.

Commentary

Again, Rodya feels crushed by Razumihkin's attentions and needs to get back to his secret world of which Razumihkin cannot be a part, and thus there is another difficult parting.

The appearance of the mysterious man who calls him a murderer is disturbing and extremely upsetting to Raskolnikov. In reality, he is the man who was present when Raskolnikov returned to the scene of the crime. He is later present when Raskolnikov returns to Porfiry's office, and he is the "hidden" fact that Porfiry keeps referring to.

After being forced to defend his theory to Porfiry and being called a murderer by the mysterious stranger, Raskolnikov is prompted by his own confusion to attempt to re-examine his theory. This re-examination reveals that he still believes strongly in the basis of his theory, but he does see that he was not good enough to execute the theory. He feels little remorse for the actual murder or death of Alyona, but instead resents the old pawnbroker as being so low that her very vileness spoils his theory. His reasoning is that if his theory is noble, it should have been tested on a noble object.

These thoughts then prompt the tenth thought of confession—this time motivated by his alternating love for his mother, yet his inability to be near her. He fears that his theory—that crime isolates a person—is working on him.

Theme

At the end of the chapter, he wonders why he always thinks of Alyona and not of Lizaveta whom he also murdered. The reason is that Alyona's murder stands for the validity of his theory. It was deliberately conceived, premeditated, and executed as a part of the theory. Therefore, his intellectual being is at stake with the murder of Alyona. But Lizaveta's murder was done out of desperation and fear and does not fit into the premeditated theory. Thus, Lizaveta's murder is no threat to his philosophical existence.

After these thoughts and hatred of the old pawnbroker, it is appropriate that he dreams of murdering the old pawnbroker again, and again, but this time he fails. It is appropriate that as he completes his dream about the murder and that at the end of this awful nightmare, the symbol of evil, Svidrigailov, appears.

Part Four
Chapter 1

Summary

Svidrigailov announces that he has come to see Raskolnikov for two reasons: First, he has long wanted to meet him, and second, he wants help in obtaining an interview with Dunya. Raskolnikov's immediate response is a negative one, and Svidrigailov begins to reveal himself freely and openly to Raskolnikov by relating many episodes of his past life. He cannot see that he has done anything wrong: He admits that once he took a riding whip to his wife Marfa Petrovna, but some women like such dominance; he admits that he did make proposals to Dunya, but many women are pleased at such attentions, and others are "highly gratified at being outraged, in spite of their pretended indignation. . .women in general love to be affronted."

This type of degenerate talk on such intimate terms prompts Raskolnikov to get up and leave at once, but his curiosity keeps him from doing so. In the midst of the conversation, Svidrigailov points out that he and Raskolnikov have a great deal in common. Raskolnikov rejects this idea, and yet he is fascinated with the talk of this admitted "vulgarian and sensualist" who is simply saturated with experiences of every kind. As Raskolnikov listens attentively and with some fascination, Svidrigailov again repeats his idea that there is "something in common" between them, a vague sense of camaraderie.

Finally, Svidrigailov announces that he wants to meet Dunya and makes her a present of 10,000 rubles so as to aid in her a rupture with Luzhin. He maintains that Dunya "is sacrificing herself, with great nobility for her family." If she does not accept his gift, she will be taking money from Luzhin anyway and would be dreadfully confined in such a cruel marriage.

Again Svidrigailov emphasizes that "there is something about you like me," and he vows if Raskolnikov does not help him arrange a meeting with Dunya, he will do so himself. As he leaves, he tells Raskolnikov that Marfa Petrovna left Dunya 3,000 rubles in her will.

Commentary

Part Four opens with the appearance of Svidrigailov to Raskolnikov. He will emerge as the epitome of the sensualist and the type of Ubermensch who is thoroughly and completely interested in the gratification of his own appetites and desires and in the assertion of his own will. He has no qualms about his activities and depends on no one. He uses his intellect only so as to aid him in obtaining sensual pleasures. In a restricted nineteenth century society, he openly discusses his sexual pleasures in a manner that identifies him as being depraved and unprincipled.

Therefore, Raskolnikov rejects his request to see Dunya because he fears this aspect of Svidrigailov and thinks that the man still has ulterior motives and designs upon Dunya. Even though Svidrigailov says that he wants to give Dunya 10,000 rubles (in today's spending value, at least fifty thousand dollars or considerably more) so that she will not have to marry Luzhin, and even though Raskolnikov believes that she is marrying Luzhin only for money, he still refuses Svidrigailov's offer of help. The mere fact that Svidrigailov makes the same point about Dunya's marriage that he had previously made, he is still offended that someone else, especially such a sensualist and vulgarian as Svidrigailov, would make that point.

Svidrigailov's repeated emphasis that there is something in common between him and Raskolnikov repulses Raskolnikov; but still he does recognize some type of affinity toward Svidrigailov, especially since the latter has made the identical point about Dunya's marriage that he had made earlier. But more centrally, the thing in common is that both men will try to assert their own will above that of others, and this aspect of the Ubermensch aligns them.

Glossary

"stamped" or "unstamped paper"   These terms would roughly be the equivalent of the American "notarized" or not. Raskolnikov's concern is not with a legal matter but instead, with the cost, however minor, of purchasing a stamp to make his declaration official.

Part Four
Chapter 2

Summary

On their way to the meeting with Luzhin, Rodya explains who Svidrigailov is and says: "I don't know why, but I am very afraid of that man." He hopes Razumihkin will help him guard Dunya from Svidrigailov, and, of course, Razumihkin agrees.

They meet Luzhin outside the apartment, and at the meeting, Luzhin relates some additional stories about Svidrigailov. They include one about his supposed seduction of a 15-year-old deaf and dumb girl who later hanged herself. Another is about Svidrigailov's servant Philip who hanged himself as a result of Svidrigailov's beatings and mockery. Luzhin concludes that Svidrigailov is the most horrible, "the most depraved, the most completely abandoned to vice" of anyone he knows. Dunya's view of each episode differs; for example, she heard that the servant Philip was addicted to drugs and that the other servants were good and loyal to Svidrigailov. Luzhin is offended that his "fiancée" seemingly defends Svidrigailov. Raskolnikov reveals that Marfa Petrovna has left Dunya 3,000 rubles, which she should receive soon.

When Rodya refuses to tell about his interview with Svidrigailov, Luzhin takes it as a personal affront and pretends he has to go. When Luzhin is confronted with the lies he wrote concerning Marmeladov's death, and Sonya's position, he is trapped and resorts to innuendo about Rodya's behavior. As the argument intensifies, Luzhin becomes more horrible and insulting until finally he insults Dunya by saying he accepted her in spite of all the unpleasant rumors about her reputation. At this, Rodya laughs, Pulcheria Alexandrovna is furious, Dunya calls him a "base, malicious person," and Razumihkin threatens him physically; Dunya then orders him to go. Even as he leaves, he is conceiving of a way to disparage Rodya and Sonya.

Commentary

The chapter presents the irony of the despicable, malicious Luzhin describing the depraved sensualist, Svidrigailov, in derogatory terms. It is questionable whether Svidrigailov is guilty of all these things, and when Dunya corrects him on a couple of matters, he perceives that she is defending him. It could not be further from the truth; Dunya is merely looking at the situation dispassionately and would be fair to anyone, even Svidrigailov whom she fears and detests. However, the prevailing stories of his rape of the blind and dumb girl and his involvement in the death of the servant does contribute to his depiction as the complete amoral sensualist.

Luzhin's nastiness comes when he reminds Dunya of his noble "resolve to take her in spite of evil rumors about her," and even though he is completely convinced that the stories are wrong, he taunts her with the rumors. Luzhin's total horror comes later when he so desperately tries to frame the innocent Sonya so as to prove himself superior to Raskolnikov.

Glossary

phalansteries Buildings similar to dormitories or communal apartment living. These were often advocated by some of the socialists.

moujiks Most translators use the word "peasants." See Constance Garnett's translation.

Toulon, Paris, Egypt, Moscow, Wilno Napoleon's decisive actions at these places were actions that confirms Napoleon as an extraordinary man.

Dussauts A famous hotel/restaurant and gathering place for advanced thinkers.

"j'ai le vin mauvais" Wine makes me belligerent (or evil). [French]

Berg A stunt person who entertained people by ascending in a balloon. Later in this chapter, Svidrigailov pretends that he will join Berg in an ascent.

"pour vous plaise" "In order to please you." [French]

Part Four
Chapter 3

Summary

Luzhin refuses to believe that such a magnificent prize as Dunya could possibly escape him. "In his dreams, he was already her lord and master," and he plans to use her mainly to forward his own career.

Meanwhile, Rodya tells his sister that Svidrigailov wants to see her and make her a present of 10,000 rubles. This offer puzzles everyone, and they decide to avoid all contact with him. Razumihkin offers a plan whereby they can all profit from the 3,000 rubles left to Dunya by Marfa Petrovna. He wants to open a small printing firm that will cater to publishing translations.

Rodya suddenly announces that he must leave. He asks pardon of his mother but insists that he is not well. As he leaves, Razumihkin follows him. Rodya is able to darkly communicate a strange secret by "some hint," and Razumihkin allows Rodya to go.

Commentary

Theme

Rodya's sudden announcement to his family that he must be alone emphasizes again the truth of his theory that crime isolates one from society, and that crime contributes to illness: "I wanted to tell you it would be better if we parted for a short time. I feel ill. I am not at peace. . . Leave me, leave me alone. . .I want to be alone; for me altogether, it's better. Don't make inquires about me. When I can, I will come of myself or . . .I will send for you. . .but if you love me, give me up. . .otherwise, I feel I shall begin to hate you."

Rodya is able to make Razumihkin know that he is implicated in the crime in some fashion. Here, then, Razumihkin's function in the novel becomes settled; he is to look after Rodya's mother and sister, thereby leaving Raskolnikov free to depart and work out his own guilt.

Part Four
Chapter 4

Summary

"Raskolnikov went straight to. . .where Sonya lived." His appearance there agitates and frightens Sonya. Rodya is stunned at how her apartment reeks of poverty and at how thin she is. As they sit together, Rodya questions her about her landlord Kapernaumov, about her profession, and then about her relationship to Katerina Ivanovna. Even though Sonya was ashamed and embarrassed with his questions, she answers with simplicity and innocence.

He then paints a horrible, depressing future life for Katerina and the children. He taunts her with the thought that Katerina will soon die—she is coughing up blood now—and the children will be left without anything. He taunts her with her inability to save any money. He taunts her with the thought that Polenka will probably have to enter also into a life of prostitution. To all of these taunts, Sonya responds with despair and dismay, and maintains that "God will not allow it to be so." To Raskolnikov's taunt that perhaps there is no God, Sonya's suffering increases because she cannot conceive of life without God.

At this point, Raskolnikov suddenly bows down to Sonya and kisses her foot, and says "I did not bow down to you, I bowed down to all the suffering of humanity." And he shocks Sonya by telling her that he did his sister honor by seating her next to his sister, "not because of your dishonor and your sin but because of your great suffering." He asks her to explain how "such shame and such baseness can exist in you side by side with other feelings, so different and so holy?" Rodya then realizes that there are only three options open to her: suicide, the madhouse, or abandonment into total debauchery.

He spots an old worn Bible on the dresser, and he is surprised to learn that it was a gift from Lizaveta who was her good friend and she has had a requiem said for Lizaveta. He asks her to read to him the story of the raising of Lazarus. She hesitates because she did not want to read to an unbeliever, but slowly and carefully, she read the story for both of them.

After she finishes reading the story, Raskolnikov tells her how much he needs her and asks her to join him and go the same road with him because they both have transgressed against life—that is Sonya has transgressed against her own self, and he has taken life. As he is about to leave, he tells Sonya that if he comes tomorrow, he will tell her who killed Lizaveta.

At the end of the chapter, we discover that Svidrigailov has been standing and listening in the next room, an empty one between his room and Sonya's. He so thoroughly enjoyed their conversation that he brings a chair so as to be more comfortable for their next meeting in which Raskolnikov has promised to reveal the murderer.

Commentary

Raskolnikov's visit to Sonya in her lodgings is in preparation for his later confession. Dostoevsky's theory that "suffering leads to salvation" and that through suffering man's sins are purified (or expiated) are now brought into the foreground. It now becomes apparent that Raskolnikov is attracted to Sonya because he sees in her the symbol and the representative of "all the suffering of humanity." Even though she is thin and frail, she can carry a very heavy burden. Thus Raskolnikov will test her further to see how much she can bear. Since she is capable of "great suffering," he torments her with taunts such as the death of Katerina, the possibility that Polenka will be forced into prostitution, and the distressing state in which she now lives. These taunts are used to test her ability to suffer intensely and ultimately to see if she will be capable of withstanding Raskolnikov's confession. Will she be able to take his suffering upon herself and help him to "bear his own cross"?

Earlier in the novel, Porfiry Petrovitch has asked Raskolnikov if he believed in the raising of Lazarus from the dead. Now he asks Sonya to read him that same story. Thus the two principal redemptive figures, Porfiry and Sonya, are both connected through the same biblical episode. A further note of coincidence is that the story is read from the

Bible that belonged to Lizaveta, the woman he did not intend to murder. The story of Lazarus is pertinent mainly in the general outline rather than in the specific detail. Raskolnikov, like Lazarus, died one type of death as a result of the crime; in other words, his crime isolated him from society and from his family to the point that he is figuratively dead. Through Christ, Lazarus was raised from the dead and became one of the living. Now through Sonya, Raskolnikov hopes to again assume his place among the living. Therefore, both stories are of people who were separated from the living and through some incredible miracle were restored to the living. The incredible aspect of the Lazarus story also appeals to Raskolnikov. The raising of Lazarus is considered one of the greatest miracles that Christ performed. In a lesser aspect, that story is one of suffering, of great suffering that was alleviated by the miracle of restoring life. Therefore, if Sonya can restore Raskolnikov to life, his suffering will be alleviated. And finally, note that Lazarus had been dead for four days before Christ performed the miracle. Likewise, it has been four days since Raskolnikov's crime.

After the reading of the story of Lazarus, Raskolnikov tells Sonya that "I have come to you because I need you." She does not understand at that moment, but he maintains that she will understand later, if not rationally then intuitively. He knows that their "paths lie together" and that they need each other as fellow sufferers to "take the suffering on ourselves."

Raskolnikov sees in Sonya one who has also transgressed against life and asks her to join him so that we "may go our way together." In asking even Sonya to join him, he symbolically breaks out of his isolation caused by the crime. Also he begins to deny that aspect of this theory that advocated the extraordinary man must stand alone and apart from all other people. But still, he has one reservation: Sonya is too much of a "religious fanatic."

Glossary

Lazarus: The story of raising of Lazarus from the dead is found in the Gospel according to John 11:1-44. There is, of course, the story of Lazarus the beggar and the rich man in Luke 16. But this story does not apply to Sonya's reading.

Part Four
Chapter 5

Summary

The day after his meeting with Sonya, Raskolnikov performs the unpleasant task of going to the Criminal Investigating section of the police department to officially file a claim to his two pawned items. He is filled with intense dread because he hated Porfiry "with an intense, unmitigated hatred" and was afraid his hatred might betray him. He is kept waiting for a long time and gets very nervous and edgy.

Porfiry receives Raskolnikov very cordially and acts as though it is a pleasant social visit, forgetting that a person is not kept waiting so long for a social visit. Raskolnikov tries to keep the meeting formal and business-like; in fact, he keeps threatening to leave unless Porfiry comes to the point and examines him in an official way. Nothing, however, seems to deter Porfiry from performing his duties his own way, and he is determined to talk about all types of subjects, especially theories about crime and crime detection.

As he talks about this and that, he paces constantly about the room and stops frequently at the door and listens to see if perhaps someone is still there. His pacing makes Raskolnikov more nervous. The interview continues for so long and is filled with so much chatter, along with irrelevances, that finally Raskolnikov loses his patience and tells Porfiry that he realizes the type of "cat and mouse game" he is playing. Raskolnikov then asserts that if he is suspected of being the murderer of "that old woman and her sister Lizaveta," then he demands to be arrested immediately or allowed to leave. "If you find that you have a legal right to prosecute me or arrest me, then do it! But I will not permit anyone to laugh in my face and torment me."

To detain Raskolnikov, Porfiry reveals that he knows many unusual things about Raskolnikov, such as his trip to the scene of the crime when he rang the doorbell and asked to see the blood. Porfiry also explains his technique: He can always arrest a person, but he prefers a suspect to have his own time to think over his crime. In Raskolnikov's case, Porfiry says that he likes him and wants to help him in a friendly manner, but Raskolnikov rejects his friendship and is about to leave when Porfiry reminds him of a little surprise that is behind the door in the next room. Before he can unlock the door, something strange and unforeseen occurs.

Commentary

Earlier, Porfiry's technique was called a "cat and mouse game." This now becomes clear to both the reader and to Raskolnikov. First, Raskolnikov is kept waiting unnecessarily; then he is exposed to incessant chatter and more chatter; and then there is the hint of some secret evidence hidden in the next room. In all these cases, Porfiry does have the upper hand, and Raskolnikov is at his mercy.

The meetings in the last two chapters show us that Raskolnikov goes from Sonya who will redeem him emotionally through her sufferings to Porfiry who will try to redeem Raskolnikov intellectually. This second redemption is more difficult since Raskolnikov's existence now is based upon the validity of his theory.

Porfiry presumably knows more than he reveals. He could arrest Raskolnikov at any time, but doesn't because he does have a "sincere liking for him" and if he arrested Raskolnikov now, Raskolnikov would never realize the error of his theory. Religiously, confession of sin is the beginning of redemption and Raskolnikov must be left alone to confess.

Glossary

tout court A French term used as an apology for a sudden undue familiarity. There is no exact term in English. Porfiry uses it to apologize for using such undue familiarity to Raskolnikov when he calls him "my dear chap" and "old Man"—phrases one would not use in addressing someone at a first meeting.

"c'est de rigueur" "It is the rule [or regulation]." [French]

"he is psychologically unable to escape me" Raskolnikov is familiar with the latest psychological terms as evidenced by his use of them here and elsewhere. Profiry uses recent terms and ideas to try to trap Raskolnikov in a series of lies or contradictions.

Part Four
Chapter 6

Summary

This chapter is told "afterwards. . .Raskolnikov recalled it this way." There was an unexpected amount of noise and the unexpected arrival of several subordinates. Porfiry is very annoyed that his plans have been interrupted, but a prisoner (Nikolay, the house painter at the scene of the crime) was brought in, and he confessed to the murder of Alyona and Lizaveta. This confession is an overwhelming surprise to both Porfiry and Raskolnikov, neither of whom expected it. Porfiry is so vexed that he is not logical and he refuses to believe it, but recovering quickly, he dismisses Raskolnikov and reminds him that they will see each other again.

Raskolnikov leaves and goes home where the strange man who had once so mysteriously appeared and called him a murderer comes and explains that he was hidden in the closet in Porfiry's office. He apologizes for calling Raskolnikov a murderer and for the trouble he has caused him. With the confession by Nikolay and the apology of the stranger, Raskolnikov resolves to make a new struggle for life.

Commentary

This six-page chapter is the shortest one in the novel. It recalls Raskolnikov's view of the incident in Porfiry's office where the house painter, Nikolay, confesses to the murder. Ironically, as Porfiry is later to know, Nikolay belongs to an unusual religious sect that emphasizes the importance of suffering for the sins of others, and his desire to suffer is the exact thing that has already been recommended for Raskolnikov.

After the porter comes to apologize for falsely accusing Raskolnikov, he decides to "make a fight for it"—a new determination to live and surpass the stupidity of his crime.

Part Five
Chapter 1

Summary

The next morning in Luzhin's rooms, he still thinks of his unfortunate break with Dunya and his thoughts are interrupted by his roommate, Lebezyatnikov, who sees himself an advanced thinker. They discuss ideas important in Russia at this time.

The discussion eventually comes around to Sonya, whom Luzhin wants to see. Luzhin insists that his roommate remain during the interview. Luzhin questions Sonya about the financial conditions of the family and about the stability of Katerina Ivanovna, who is telling people that Luzhin is going to arrange for a pension for her. Luzhin makes it clear that he has no influence, but he tells Sonya he would like to try to get some type of fund started for the widowed Katerina. To show his good intent, he gives Sonya a ten-ruble note.

Commentary

Most of this chapter is a digression that allows Dostoevsky to examine some of the prominent advanced ideas of the time—ideas that were influencing such people as Raskolnikov and to a much lesser degree, the simplistic Lebezyatnikov, whom Dostoevsky depicts as an advanced liberal and a comic rube. Basically, these discussions show Dostoevsky's extreme dislike and distrust for the radical young men who are too influenced by new ideas. The foolishness of Lebezyatnikov is supposedly the foolishness of any person who adheres so closely to the "advanced ideas."

Regarding the development of the plot, this chapter merely sets up the proper machinery for Luzhin's attempt to frame Sonya.

Part Five
Chapter 2

Summary

At Katerina Ivanovna's, the funeral party is just beginning. The dinner was given so as to "do like other people." The party far exceeds Katerina's means to pay, but she insisted on inviting everyone, even her landlady, Amalia Fyodorovna Lippewechsel, whom she dislikes intensely; Lebezyatnikov who once beat her; and Luzhin whom she does not know.

When Katerina notices that many people, especially the more genteel and influential lodgers, turned down her invitation, she blames it on her landlady and begins to act disdainful and haughty around her. Sonya is quiet, very nervous, and apprehensive, but Raskolnikov says nothing. Then as the party progresses, Katerina becomes openly critical and then hostile toward the landlady as though she was responsible for all the misfortunes in Katerina's life. Finally, pandemonium breaks loose and the entrance of Luzhin prevents an open fight.

Commentary

In this chapter, Katerina's behavior predicts her forthcoming eviction and her death. She cannot control herself, and she is also spitting blood. Her behavior is irrational as in her open prejudice against her landlady, Amalia Ivanovna Lippewechsel, a person of German origin who (in some translations) speaks in a heavy German syntax. Katerina's irrational dislike stems from a long standing conflict between native Russians and members of the German working class who settled in Russia but seldom learned the Russian language.

While Raskolnikov is physically present at this party, his real presence is unobserved; that is, he is no more than another visitor. His importance will be in the next chapter when he witnesses Luzhin's disgraceful and vicious attempts at blackmailing Sonya.

Part Five
Chapter 3

Summary

Katerina Ivanovna is excited to see Luzhin, thinking he has suddenly become her savior, but she is struck dumb when he disclaims all knowledge of her father and he stands disdainfully apart from her and avoids her as much as possible.

Luzhin then announces the purpose of his visit; he has come to see Sonya. Shortly afterwards, Lebezyatnikov appears at the back of the room and remains quietly there. Luzhin explains loudly to Sonya how he had exchanged some securities for rubles, and that when she left the room after their interview, a one-hundred ruble note was missing. He carefully explains that he had just counted the money and one of the notes is now missing. He accuses Sonya of black ingratitude and demands that she return the money. Sonya denies the charge, and Katerina immediately comes to her defense. Luzhin threatens to send for the police, but tells Sonya that if she will return the note, he will forget everything. Katerina then becomes enraged and screams for someone to search her. As Katerina begins frantically to turn Sonya's pockets inside out, a hundred ruble note falls out of one of the pockets. Sonya still denies the theft, and the landlady orders them from the house.

Lebezyatnikov steps forward and accuses Luzhin of being a vile, evil person. He tells how he saw Luzhin slip the hundred-ruble note into Sonya's pocket while she was standing in his room, amazed at the fact that he had given her ten rubles. Luzhin denies the accusation, and Lebezyatnikov is at a loss to explain why Luzhin acted as he did.

At this moment, Raskolnikov steps forward and explains how Luzhin was rejected by his sister and he tried to alienate him from his family by implicating Sonya. At this time, Luzhin leaves as quickly as possible, but someone throws a glass at him. The glass misses Luzhin, but it hits the landlady who in turn orders Katrina out of the house. Sonya could endure no more and "she gave way to hysteria" and hurried home. Raskolnikov follows her wondering what she can say now about her predicament.

Commentary

From the wild, frantic scene in Chapter 2, we move to a quieter but more intense chapter where we see Luzhin's attempt to frame Sonya. His elaborate preparations to prove her to be a thief indicate his desperation, his vileness, and his amoral stance. His attempt to disgrace her is only so as to cast aspersion upon Raskolnikov, thereby hoping to prove to Dunya that he was right in his judgment about Raskolnikov's relationship to Sonya. He is ultimately the most despicable person in the novel, and this scene proves that Raskolnikov was right in strongly opposing Dunya's marriage to him.

Sonya leaves before the horror of the scene is over. When she goes to her own room to escape Katerina's hysteria, Amalia Ivanovna's anger, and the general air of disillusionment, she intuitively knows that Raskolnikov will follow her. Note that Raskolnikov watches Sonya's behavior and concludes that "she was capable of bearing everything. . .with patience and serenity."

Glossary

kutya A ceremonial dish most commonly served at funerals along with other delicacies.

pancakes A translator today would use the Russian word *blintzes*, which is now a familiar part of English cooking terminology and belongs both to the Russian and the Yiddish cultures.

samovar A metal urn with a spigot and an internal tube for heating water in making tea: used esp. in Russia.

"en toutes lettres" "[printed] in all capital letters." Katerina Ivanovna is proud of her schooling with a certificate that has her name printed in large letters. [French]

"Geld" "Money"; the rent money has not been paid.

"Gott der Barmherzige!" A cry of exasperation that has no exact English translation: the closest would be "Oh, merciful God." The point is that Amalia Ivanovna, when provoked, curses in German not Russian.

Part Five
Chapter 4

Summary

On his way to see Sonya, Raskolnikov wonders if it is absolutely necessary to tell Sonya who killed Lizaveta. When she meets him, she had indeed been waiting for him and she pleads that he not talk to her the way he did yesterday—"there is enough misery in the world." But Raskolnikov ignores her plea and immediately reminds her of the things that he had said yesterday.

Over her protests, Raskolnikov asks her a hypothetical question—that is, between Luzhin and Katerina, which one should be allowed to go on living? Should Luzhin live and continue committing acts of evil and hate crimes and causing the imprisonment of people like Sonya and the deaths of Katerina and the children? Or should Katerina Ivanovna go on living? "How do you decide? Which of them should die?" Sonya refuses to answer saying "I can't know God's intentions? Why do you ask such questions that have no answer? Who am I to judge who shall live and who shall not?" As Raskolnikov asks these difficult questions, Sonya realizes his suffering and asks what is troubling him.

Raskolnikov reminds Sonya that he had promised to tell her today who killed Lizaveta. To Sonya's frightened response, he first asks her to guess and then tells her to "take a good look at me." Somehow the dreadful knowledge is communicated to Sonya and all of her suffering suddenly becomes magnified. She shrinks from Raskolnikov. Recovering immediately, she flings herself on her knees in front of him, crying out: "What have you done, what have you done to yourself?. . . .There is no one, no one unhappier than you in the whole world."

A sudden feeling of tenderness floods Rodya's heart and softens it, and he asks Sonya: "Do not forsake me." and she vows she will "Never, forsake you, nowhere! . . . I will follow you wherever you go. . . I will even follow you to prison." At the mention of prison or Siberia, Raskolnikov recoils, and his haughty attitude returns.

When Sonya asks him how he could bring himself to do such a thing, Raskolnikov offers explanations ranging from his poverty to his Ubermensch theory. Each of his reasons is rejected so that Raskolnikov never successfully explains his crime. After many attempts to explain the crime, he turns to Sonya and asks "tell me what to do now?" She requests him "Go at once, this very minute, stand at the cross-roads, bow down, first kiss the earth which you have defiled [desecrated] and then bow down to the whole world and say to all men aloud, 'I am a murderer!'"

When Rodya questions this, she tells him again: "Accept suffering and achieve atonement through it." Rodya hedges still and asks Sonya if she will come and visit him in prison, and as she affirms that she will, she offers him the cypress-wood cross that was once Lizaveta's. He reaches for it, but decides it would be better if he accepted it later, and Sonya agrees: "When you accept your suffering, you shall put it on."

At this crucial moment, Lebezyatnikov rushes into the room.

Commentary

The idea of "suffering" becomes uppermost at this point. It is as if Sonya has not suffered enough, Raskolnikov deliberately increases her suffering first by pointing out that Katerina and the children are now homeless. Then after he has seen the very depth of her suffering, he then prepares her for his confession of the murder.

By way of preparation for his confession, or more important, his assuaging his own guilt or complicity, he asks Sonya the hypothetical question of whether Luzhin or Katerina should live. Sonya bases her refusal to answer upon her reliance on Divine Providence: "How can I know the will of God?" Hence, she simply will not entertain such an idea.

After many attempts and thoughts of confession (at least ten times) Raskolnikov almost makes an open confession, but he cannot yet formulate his crime into words. He can only hint and then say "Take a good look." Now and all through this chapter, Sonya is aware that Raskolnikov is suffering tremendously and his suffering increases hers. She is aware that the suffering is a path to expiation and redemption.

After the confession, Sonya promises that she will follow him to Siberia. This is not just an idle promise; she takes part of Raskolnikov's suffering upon herself. As soon as Sonya mentions Siberia, Raskolnikov again attempts to explain, rationalize, or justify the murders. He rejects each attempt as soon as he offers it. As pointed out earlier, he was forced by circumstances to commit the murder before his theory was completely formulated. Now as he attempts to explain it, he realizes how incomplete it really was. This realization is seen in the fact that as soon as he offers a reason, he then rejects it with the words: "No, No, that wasn't it." This is repeated so often that it functions as a thematic motif throughout the scene.

His reasons for the murder include: it was merely for plunder, he wanted to be a type of Napoleon, he needed money to keep himself in school without being a burden to his mother, he killed only a louse, he was being vain and mad, and he wanted to see if he had the daring to do it.

Sonya's advice to Raskolnikov is to suffer and expiate his sin, "to go at once, this very minute, stand at the cross-roads" and confess. Raskolnikov rejects this because he fears the laughter of men who would call him a coward and a fool—a coward because he couldn't live by his ideas, and a fool because he would follow the advice of a prostitute. Sonya also wants him to wear the wooden cross, but he rejects it until a later date because he was not quite prepared to acknowledge completely his crime.

A mystery in this chapter is where and when did Sonya get Lizaveta's cypress cross?

Glossary

Gaol The British spelling for jail or prison. Most translations use British forms and terminology.

Siberia Geographically, Siberia is the large frozen land mass in the most northern part of Russia. In common speech, it refers to the infamous prisons of Northern Russia.

"No Toulon, no Egypt, no crossing of Mont Blanc" These are some of Napoleon's great feats that characterize him as one of the extraordinary men of the world.

Part Five
Chapter 5

Summary

Lebezyatnikov has come with the information that Katerina has been evicted from her apartment, has gone mad, and is now wandering madly around the town with the children dressed in outlandish and absurd costumes. She is forcing them to sing and beg from strangers. Her speech is virtually incoherent, and her behavior is incomprehensible. Sonya rushes to her but suddenly, Rodya feels repulsed by Sonya and questions himself why he had come to her.

Raskolnikov returns to his room where he finds Dunya waiting for him. She explains that she better understands his situation because Razumihkin explained how Raskolnikov is troubled by the police and their false suspicions. She offers him her complete loyalty and love and will come to him any time that he needs her. Raskolnikov longs to tell Dunya the truth but cannot.

As Raskolnikov wanders aimlessly about the city, he comes upon Katerina. She has attracted a large crowd who have gathered to watch and laugh at her crazy antics. She is forcing the children to beg and, is arguing with strangers on the streets, and is trying to force her way into strange houses. Then as she runs through the streets, she stumbles, falls, and cuts herself. She is carried to Sonya's room nearby. A doctor is sent for, but Katerina is dying. She maintains that she needs no priest or doctor, and as she dies, Svidrigailov, who lives in the next room, enters and volunteers to undertake all of the arrangements. He tells Raskolnikov that he will use the money that he was going to give to Dunya to apply it to the care the children and will settle a large sum upon Sonya also.

By using the exact phrasing and terms that Raskolnikov used in making his confession to Sonya, he thus subtly reveals to Raskolnikov that he overheard the entire conversation between him and Sonya, and he reminds Raskolnikov that "I told you that we should come together again—I foretold it."

Commentary

The dual aspect of Raskolnikov's personality is exemplified again when Raskolnikov is drawn to Sonya enough to make his confession, but after having done so, he is suddenly repulsed by her. Part of his repulsion is due to the fact that he dislikes her ideas about suffering and more importantly that he needs to go to prison.

In addition to confessing to Sonya, he also wants to confess his crime to his sister. The idea of confession has been constantly with Raskolnikov since moments after the murder.

The death of Katerina leaves Sonya responsible for the children. Rodya had foretold this to Sonya and now it is true. Consequently, Svidrigailov shows up, and the money he had once intended for Dunya will now go to Sonya and the children, which will free Sonya financially to follow Raskolnikov to Siberia.

Glossary

"Tenez-nous droite!" "Let's stand up tall" The upper class in Russia spoke fluent French. Here in this situation, Katerina Ivanovna's use of French is somewhat out of place and affected.

Part Six
Chapter 1

Summary

It was a strange time for Raskolnikov: Katerina Ivanovna is dead; Dunya has visited him; Svidrigailov, who had overheard his conversation with Sonya, worries him the most. Now Razumihkin comes to accuse him of being a scoundrel for ignoring his family. He informs Rodya that his mother, Pulcheria Alexandrovna, had come to see him thinking he was sick but eventually decided he had forgotten his mother.

Razumihkin is disgusted with Rodya until he hears about Dunya's visit and that Rodya wants him to look after both Dunya and her mother: "Whatever happens to me, wherever I go, you will stay and look after them. I entrust them to you." Razumihkin also tells Rodya that Dunya received a strange letter that upset her greatly. Just before Razumihkin leaves, he tells Rodya that Porfiry, using very complicated psychological terms, explained how the painter confessed to the murder, and again Raskolnikov wonders if Porfiry is again playing the "cat and mouse" game. At this moment, Porfiry knocks at the door.

Commentary

Theme

Here the fresh air motif reappears. The need for fresh air is one of the supposed reasons for Raskolnikov's illness.

With the appearance of Razumihkin, Raskolnikov makes a further dispensation for the care of his family; that is, Razumihkin will look after them, which leaves Rodya free for the actions he is about to take. The money that Marfa Petrovna left to Dunya will free them; the money that Svidrigailov is going to invest for the children and the money he is leaving Sonya frees her first of the children and sets her free to follow Rodya.

The mention of the mysterious letter that Dunya received will be clarified later as being from Svidrigailov. From thoughts of Svidrigailov, Raskolnikov is immediately confronted with Porfiry. Whereas in earlier meetings with Porfiry, Raskolnikov had been frightened and intimidated by him, now "he was scarcely afraid of him." The point is that Raskolnikov has now made contact with humanity again through his confession to Sonya, and therefore is no longer of afraid of being trapped in the "cat and mouse" game.

Part Six
Chapter 2

Summary

Porfiry begins rattling on about these poisoned cigarettes, and Raskolnikov wonders if Porfiry is going to play the same old game again. He
throws Raskolnikov off guard by apologizing for their last meeting—"it
was such a strange scene"—and perhaps he acted unfairly. He wants to
convince Raskolnikov that he is sincerely attracted to him, and he
believes that Raskolnikov is "a most honorable man with elements of
greatness in him." Furthermore, he possesses a noble soul and elements
of magnanimity.

Porfiry also wants to explain all the various circumstances that led
him to think Raskolnikov is the murderer—the pledges, the theory, the
illness, the return to the scene of the crime, and other matters. He then
explains why Nikolay the painter confessed to the murder. The painter
happens to belong to an old religious order, which believes that man
should suffer and to suffer at the hands of authorities is the best type
of suffering, but above all "simply suffering is necessary."

At the end of his narration, Porfiry then explains how Nikolay could
not have committed the murder. Instead, after describing the events
surrounding the murder, he announces, "you Rodion Romanovitch,
you are the murderer." After making this accusation, Porfiry tells him
that he will not arrest him for several days because he wants Raskolnikov to come of his own volition and openly make the confession. To
arrest him "is not to my interest."

Porfiry then tells Raskolnikov why he likes him and advises Raskolnikov to learn to love life, not to scorn the possibility of a mitigation of
sentence. Likewise, he advises Raskolnikov to suffer "because suffering
is a great thing." Before he leaves, Porfiry announces that he has no fear
Raskolnikov might be tempted to run away; therefore, he is quite safe
in letting him remain free until he confesses.

Commentary

First, even though Porfiry is able to explain so much, the reader must step back and acknowledge that the information that Rodion Romanovitch is the murderer is still only circumstantial evidence and in modern courts would be insufficient to bring about a conviction.

Porfiry's explanation of the crime and his refusal to arrest Raskolnikov show that he does sincerely like Raskolnikov, but more importantly he also believes in Raskolnikov's greatness. Porfiry's true purpose and mission becomes clear in this chapter. First, one must understand that Porfiry, like Dostoevsky, was a dedicated Slavophil, one who believes that the Slavic people are a type of "chosen people." In other words, Porfiry believed so strongly in the greatness of Russia that he is constantly searching and helping those who he thinks will be the future leaders of Russia or who will be able to contribute to Russia's greatness in other ways. Therefore, he views Raskolnikov as a man of noble character, one of the young intellects of Russia who could be of great service to the state if he learns to reject his radical ideas. Porfiry attempts to force Raskolnikov to acknowledge that his theory is wrong, and from this confession to go on and face life and become one of the most important minds of Russia. If Porfiry were to arrest Raskolnikov immediately, it would ruin Raskolnikov's intellectual redemption through self-realization. But if Porfiry gives Raskolnikov enough time to confess on his own (and thus realize and acknowledge to himself his own error), then Raskolnikov will achieve a greatness in his own right. Therefore, it would be no advantage to arrest Raskolnikov unless it is for simple punishment, and Porfiry has greater things in mind for Raskolnikov than punishment; he wants redemption and greatness from Rodya.

Raskolnikov's confession earlier to Sonya represents one aspect of his character and Sonya is trying to redeem Raskolnikov by asking him to take up his cross and suffer. As a parallel, Porfiry also emphasizes the importance of suffering, which accounts for Nikolay's confession, but Porfiry emphasizes the importance of suffering as a means of expiation, "for suffering, Rodion Romanovitch, is a great thing."

Glossary

"umsonst" "in vain." [German]

Part Six
Chapter 3

Summary

After Porfiry's pronouncement, Raskolnikov hurries to Svidrigailov's. He feels that the man has some power over him, a feeling he cannot understand. At the same time he feels some repulsion toward Sonya and thinks that he must go his own way or hers.

As he walks towards Svidrigailov's room, he wonders if the man has talked to Porfiry and decides that he hasn't. He suddenly sees Svidrigailov in a restaurant. Svidrigailov appears as though he was anxious not to be seen or as if he was trying to avoid him, but he finally calls to Raskolnikov to join him.

Raskolnikov immediately warns Svidrigailov to stop all attempts to see Dunya and threatens to kill him if he tries again. Due to the overheard conversation between Sonya and him, Svidrigailov should know that Raskolnikov is capable of murder and will certainly carry out his threat. Svidrigailov pretends to be interested only in becoming better acquainted with Raskolnikov and in learning from him about the new ideas and new ways of enjoying oneself. Suddenly Raskolnikov feels oppressed by Svidrigailov's talk of debauchery and sensuality, and he begins to leave.

Commentary

Character Insight

Soon after his confession to Sonya, Raskolnikov is drawn to Svidrigailov without realizing that Svidrigailov represents one aspect of his character. Svidrigailov, since their first meeting, has frequently asserted that there was something in common between them. These thoughts cause him to be somewhat repulsed by the thought of Sonya. "He was afraid of Sonya. . .he must go his own way or hers." But Raskolnikov is also convinced that his and Svidrigailov's "evil-doings could not be of the same kind."

Part Six
Chapter 4

Summary

Svidrigailov persuades Raskolnikov to remain a while longer and he tells how his wife Marfa rescued him from debtor's prison, and knowing that he had a wandering eye, made him agree to a verbal contract where she was to be informed of his various "wandering eyes." He did often flirt with the hired help until Dunya reprimanded him. When Dunya grew sorry for him, he knew he had a chance with her because she was the type of woman who could enjoy being martyred. As he tells the story of his seduction of a faithful wife, Raskolnikov becomes more and more disgusted, especially when he speaks of how "Dunya's eyes can flash fire." When he tells of all the intimate details of his 15-year-old fiancée who would often cuddle in his lap and then confesses that in his own debauchery he likes "my sewers to be filthy," Raskolnikov's repulsion is too much. He departs this "vile, nasty, depraved, sensual man."

Commentary

Svidrigailov is a consummate artist in the ways of seduction, and he horrifies Raskolnikov with his descriptions. The modern reader must realize that in the latter part of the nineteenth century all of Europe had a period of great prudery and restraint. For a person to talk as Svidrigailov did, even though today it seems harmless, was a horrible shocking matter. To discuss Dunya in sexual terms to the brother is an indescribable violation of decency. For Svidrigailov to regale himself in these vividly realized scenes characterizes him as an exceptionally vulgar person. And yet, in the final analysis, how can a murderer find a horrible fault in a sensualist?

Even though Raskolnikov cannot yet see what draws him to Svidrigailov, he is finally able to see what it is in Svidrigailov that disgusts him and sets him apart—it is his vile sensuality that makes him so vulgar and depraved.

Part Six
Chapter 5

Summary

Raskolnikov fears that Svidrigailov still has evil designs on his sister and is determined to follow him. Svidrigailov is disgusted and annoyed because the designated time to meet Dunya has almost elapsed. Therefore, he begins to bring up the subject of the murder and to make caustic remarks to Raskolnikov calling him a romantic (Schillerresque Romantic) who objects to people listening at doors but it's alright to murder an old louse. Finally, Raskolnikov is disgusted with being around Svidrigailov and he leaves.

As he walks away he passes Dunya but does not see her. At the same time Dunya sees Svidrigailov waiting for her and she hurriedly goes to meet him. Svidrigailov tricks Dunya into his room by hinting about strange things Raskolnikov has done and also by assuring her that all the neighbors, including Sonya, will be present.

In his room he reveals to her all that he has heard about Raskolnikov's confession. He explains how Raskolnikov committed the crime to support some theories of his. As he explains the theories, Dunya is able to believe him because she has carefully read the article that Raskolnikov published about his theories of crime and the criminal. Svidrigailov then suggests that Raskolnikov get a ticket to some place far away, maybe America, because Raskolnikov "may yet be a great man." After he convinces her of her brother's guilt, he then reveals that only she can save her brother by submitting to his seduction.

Dunya quickly rushes to the door and finds it locked. Svidrigailov reveals that the other tenants, including Sonya, are away and will not return until late at night. Svidrigailov implores Dunya to submit to the seduction even though he points out how easily it would be for him to overpower her; she is at his mercy. She would not be able to complain to the authorities without implicating and finally condemning her own brother.

At this time, Dunya pulls out a gun that Svidrigailov recognizes as belonging to him; she had taken it long ago when she was the governess. Svidrigailov begins to threateningly approach Dunya. She shoots once and misses. She shoots once more and the bullet grazes his hair. Svidrigailov does not rush Dunya; instead, he gives her all the time she needs in order to reload the pistol. He is willing to let Dunya kill him. After she has reloaded the pistol, he approaches her again saying that this time at three paces, she can hardly miss, but she can't fire and she drops the pistol. Svidrigailov feels that this is a good sign. He takes her in his arms and asks her if she can love him. To her response of "Never," he then gives her the key and tells her to take it but make haste and leave. Svidrigailov remains a few minutes longer, and then takes his hat and leaves.

Commentary

At the beginning of the chapter, Raskolnikov is suspicious that Svidrigailov still has plans to seduce Dunya and resolves to follow him. Ironically, he is completely right. Svidrigailov knows this, but he is also shrewd enough to know that Raskolnikov can't stomach his vulgar talk. True to form, Raskolnikov suddenly is repulsed and disgusted with the man's depravity and cannot stand to be in his presence any longer.

The scene with Dunya is the most crucial in Svidrigailov's life. Prior to this scene, Svidrigailov had functioned as a man completely self-sufficient, needing no one. Like Raskolnikov, he thought that his aims and desires were above those of the ordinary man. Likewise, in the past, whenever Svidrigailov wanted something, he simply took it and defied all consequences. He lived with the idea that he needed no one and that he could withstand all things. Now he finds that he not only wants Dunya, but also, and more importantly, he wants Dunya to want him. Here then, is the total failure of the Ubermensch—that is, the total impossibility of man's being able to exist completely alone.

If it were only the sensual pleasure derived from seducing Dunya, Svidrigailov could have easily raped her. If it were a matter of simply asserting his self-will and power, he could have easily done that. Previously, Svidrigailov had dared to face life alone—that is, to measure his will against all things. In doing this he has been utterly alone—in complete solitude as Raskolnikov was. He has committed evil so that he might know whether some power beyond him could punish him, and he has not been punished. So there is nothing for his unconquerable will to will any more. His is a loneliness that is more than he can bear. He then turns to Dunya knowing that she dislikes him, yet hoping there may be a spark of love behind all the loathing that would show him he is not alone. Twice she fires at him. He remains and allows her to fire so as to see if he can be punished. But before she fires a third time, she drops the pistol. The one last hope for himself is aroused. "A weight seemed to have rolled from his heart. . .it was the deliverance from another feeling, darker and more bitter, which he could not himself define." This feeling is the hope that Dunya's dropping of the gun means that she can give freely of herself to him; he asks if she loves him or can ever love him. Never. That hope is destroyed, and he is again completely alone. He has crossed the bounds of all human experience in his desire to find whether the burden of life rests on his will alone or whether there is something beyond, and he has found nothing. Death then is the only thing that he has left untried—the only thing he has not yet willed. It is for him to finally will his own death.

Glossary

"I suppose [Razumihkin] is a seminarist" Svidrigailov thinks that Razumihkin is a student in a seminary studying for the priesthood. The Literary Monuments Edition maintains that Razumihkin's name is similar to the names typically given by bishops to graduates of seminaries upon their completing the school, at which time they are often assigned new names.

"cher ami" "dear friend." For Svidrigailov to call Raskolnikov "cher ami" is patronizing and insulting. [French]

"La nature et la verite" This means to be natural and truthful. [French]

"Ou va-t-elle la vertu nicher" "Where does one go to conceal herself in virtue." [French]

"the Schiller in you" Schiller is a German romantic poet. His name is attached to things noble, good, and worthwhile. A "Schiller-like" person would never stoop to Svidrigailov's vulgarity.

"une theorie comme une autre" "One theory is like another one." [French]

Part Six
Chapter 6

Summary

After Dunya's departure, Svidrigailov indulges his low, vulgar taste in entertainment places on his way to Sonya's room, next door to his. He tells her that Katerina's three children are very well taken care of. He then gives her 3,000 rubles for her own use. When she tries to refuse, he tells her of Raskolnikov's two alternatives—either a bullet through the head or prison in Siberia. There is only one qualification for accepting the money; she is to tell absolutely no one where it came from. Also she should take it tomorrow or as soon as possible and deposit it with Razumihkin.

Svidrigailov continues on his way to see his 15-year-old fiancée and leaves her a note for 15,000 rubles. Returning now to his room, he dreams of finding a young five-year-old girl whom he picks up and takes to his room. In his dream, this girl suddenly grows older and assumes the role of a depraved French prostitute. Svidrigailov then gets up and wanders to the park where he takes out his revolver and puts a bullet through his head.

Commentary

After Dunya's declaration that she could never love him, Svidrigailov realized that he needed more than sensual pleasure; he also needed human warmth and affection. His entire life was based on the theory that he was completely self-sufficient and self-contained, that he needed no one, that whatever he wanted he would simply take and ignore any consequences, and that his will was stronger than anything else.

Suddenly with his realization that he needed but could not will the human warmth Dunya could supply, he saw the failure and sham of his previous existence. With this insight, he simply cannot return to his previous mode of existence, which he realized to be false. Likewise, he cannot change. The only thing he has not willed so far is his own death. Immediately after these realizations, he has the dream about the little girl he picked up and who, under his touch, turns into a shameless whore. Thus, these realizations lead him to his suicide. Svidrigailov feels there is no other choice for him except to will his own death.

Theme

Svidrigailov's suicide is part of Dostoevsky's thesis that no man can set himself apart from humanity. There can be no superman, no Ubermensch, who is allowed to transgress the law. Sooner or later, every person needs human warmth and companionship.

Glossary

Vauxhall Originally this was a famous restaurant with music dating back to the seventeenth century. It was so popular that the name Vauxhall came to stand for any outdoor restaurant and attached gardens throughout Europe.

Café chantant A musical type of café but with more risqué music.

"A cannon shot. . . Ah! The signal." The Neva River runs through St. Petersburg and the city was often subjected to flooding. The cannon shot warns the citizens that a flood might be approaching.

Part Six
Chapter 7

Summary

On that same day that Svidrigailov commits suicide, Rodya is on way to pay his last visit to this mother. She is alone. She refuses to question him about his whereabouts and maintains that she has read his article three times and feels that he is destined for greatness. She states that she will not interfere. He tells her "I came to assure you that I have always loved you, and now I am glad that we are alone." Again and again, he assures her of his abiding love for her, but also tells her that he has to go away for a long time. However, before he leaves, he asks his mother "to kneel down and pray to God for me. Your prayers perhaps will reach Him." She makes the cross over him and blesses him, and he leaves promising that someday he will return to her.

When he returns to his room, he finds Dunya waiting for him. She has been all day with Sonya waiting for him. Dunya now knows of the crime and agrees that it was wrong but is proud that he "is ready to face suffering." She, like Sonya and Porfiry, also believes that he expiates his crime "by facing his suffering." Still Raskolnikov cannot bring himself to admit the crime as evil: "Crime? What crime?. . .Killing a foul, noxious louse, that old moneylender, no good to anybody, who sucked the life-blood of the poor, so vile that killing her ought to bring absolution for forty sins."

He only admits that it was his own baseness, his incompetence, and clumsiness that were at fault. But he assures Dunya that he is ready to take his suffering even though he can see no value to it. He also promises that he shall be honorable and manly and that some day, she will hear him spoken of favorably. As he leaves, he asks himself why is he going to Sonya's house now. He feels he has already made her suffer too much, but all the same he goes.

Commentary

Character Insight

The scene between mother and son shows a new side of Rodya. Since they are alone, a very important fact to him, he is able to freely express his love for his mother—a thing that he has earlier found tedious, confining, and a violation of his theory of the superior man. In this highly charged emotional scene, he is able to not only express his love to his mother, but he is also able to ask her to pray for him. This change is a sign that he is beginning his redemption.

In his last talk with Dunya, she also emphasizes the saving quality of suffering. But again, Raskolnikov revolts against this basic idea. He still has an intellectual belief in the idea that provoked the crime. His only regret is that he has disgraced the nobility of the idea because he, as a person, is cowardly and contemptible.

Part Six
Chapter 8

Summary

Dunya and Sonya had been waiting all day for Rodya, fearing that he might have taken his life. Dunya gives up and goes to Rodya's room to wait for him. When he arrives at Sonya's, she is overjoyed to see him. He immediately tells her "I have come for your crosses—it was you who sent me to the cross-roads." As she goes for the crosses, he decides that he will not go to Porfiry because he is sick of him.

Sonya returns with the crosses, makes the sign of the cross over him, and hangs the little cypress-wood cross on his breast. He then tells Sonya, "This then is a symbol that I am taking up my cross." At Sonya's fervent request, he makes the "sign of the cross several times" and Sonya gets her shawl to accompany him, but he tells her he has to go alone. She follows discreetly but remains at a distance in the shadows.

As he goes to confess, he does not understand Sonya's grief since he is doing what she had asked. But he remembers her advice to go to the cross-roads and as he kneels and kisses the ground, a roar of laughter erupts from all who were around him. Some thought he was drunk; others thought him mad. He is about to abandon the entire idea and then he sees Sonya in the shadows at a distance. "In that moment Raskolnikov knew in his heart, once and for all, that Sonya would be with him for always, and would follow him to the ends of the earth."

He enters the police station and asks for Zametov, who is not there and he has to listen to some ravings from Ilya Petrovitch. Suddenly Raskolnikov overhears that Svidrigailov has shot himself. Without making his confession, he turns to go out and once on the steps he sees Sonya standing in the distance. He turns and goes back and tells the official: "It was I who killed the old pawnbroker woman and her sister Lizaveta with an axe and robbed them."

Commentary

Raskolnikov's last visit to Sonya shows his intentions to "take up his cross" and begin his re-entry into humanity. When he has taken on the cypress-wood cross, he makes the sign of the cross for Sonya's sake, which is a step toward redemption. It is the wooden cross and not the copper one, saving the latter for another day.

In his suffering, he also sees that Sonya suffers. As he goes to make his confession, he remembers her words to "Bow down to the people, kiss the earth, and say aloud, I am a murderer." As he begins to do these, he immediately provokes laughter; earlier his pride prevented him from becoming an object of ridicule of the people and still he has his fear of being laughed at because he still has a strong belief in the validity of his theory.

At the police station, he hates to confess to the supercilious Ilya Petrovitch, but with Zametov gone, and Ilya prattling on in a silly fashion, the news that Svidrigailov has shot himself causes him to leave the station without making a confession. As he leaves the station, the sight of Sonya, the symbol of suffering humanity, causes him to return. And with the confession, the novel comes to a thematic close. The confession is a culmination of the many attempts at confession that he has contemplated since his murder of the pawnbroker and her sister.

Glossary

"Nihil est" "Nothing is." The name *nihilism* comes from this; this is an allusion to the negativism of that movement. [Latin]

Epilogue

Summary

The epilogue takes place in a prison in Siberia, eighteen months after the day of the murder and nine months after Rodion Raskolnikov had been confined in the prison.

At the trial, the fact that Raskolnikov made a voluntary confession, that he had never counted the money or spent any, that he was on the verge of a mental breakdown, that he didn't profit personally from the crime, that many witnesses testified to his unusual behavior and also to the general nobility of his character and that he had often performed many charitable acts all combine to soften his sentence. Raskolnikov's mother fell ill during the trial and was never informed of her son's crime and his sentence. Raskolnikov is sentenced to eight years in Siberia. With the money left by Svidrigailov, Sonya is able to make preparations to follow him to Siberia. Two months after the trial, Dunya and Razumihkin are married.

In the prison, Raskolnikov is sullen and distant. He will have nothing to do with the other prisoners. He is antagonistic about Sonya. Then suddenly, he is taken ill and put into the hospital. He re-examines his theories and still considers them to be right even though he blundered. He has not seen Sonya for a long time. When he finds out that Sonya is ill and unable to leave her apartment, he is finally able to see her again. He realizes how much she means to him. At this time, he realizes also that even though he still has seven more years of suffering ahead of him, he will have even more years of infinite happiness head of him.

Commentary

Historically, Russia had three types of prisoners: The most severe criminal received life imprisonment or a term of more than 12 years. The second class received an imprisonment of 8 to 12 years and the third class received less than 8 years. Raskolnikov, therefore, receives the lightest possible sentence for the second class. All three classes had to work in the mines, but the severity was in relationship to class and other matters.

Most critics and readers of this novel consider the end of Part Six to be the most logical place for the novel to end. However, nineteenth century fiction dictated a final summary, or epilogue.

Certainly, nothing essential or new is given here and all the motifs and symbols suggest that Raskolnikov is now on his way towards becoming a fully integrated personality. The Epilogue seems to be a device used to satisfy the average person and is essentially superfluous to the novel. In the typical fashion of the nineteenth century novel, the Epilogue simply "tidies up" loose ends. For example, Dostoevsky tells us that Dunya and Razumihkin are married, and that Sonya follows Raskolnikov to Siberia. These two facts were quite apparent to the readers without being flatly told again in the Epilogue. Likewise, we also find out that Sonya brings about Raskolnikov's final redemption simply by her quiet unassuming presence and her willingness to serve him and suffer with him. But this also we know from the interviews that Raskolnikov and Sonya had together. Therefore, the formal structure of the novel ends with Raskolnikov's confession at the police station.

CHARACTER ANALYSES

The following critical analyses delve into the physical, emotional, and psychological traits of the literary work's major characters so that you might better understand what motivates these characters. The writer of this study guide provides this scholarship as an educational tool by which you may compare your own interpretations of the characters. Before reading the character analyses that follow, consider first writing your own short essays on the characters as an exercise by which you can test your understanding of the original literary work. Then, compare your essays to those that follow, noting discrepancies between the two. If your essays appear lacking, that might indicate that you need to re-read the original literary work or re-familiarize yourself with the major characters.

Rodion Romanovitch Raskolnikov

Raskolnikov is best seen as two characters. He sometimes acts in one manner and then suddenly in a manner completely contradictory. These actions compel one to view him as having a split personality or as being a dual character. Perhaps the best description of Raskolnikov occurs in Part Three, Chapter 2 when Razumihkin tries to explain to Raskolnikov's mother, Pulcheria Alexandrovna, and to his sister, Dunya (Avdotya Romanovna) how Raskolnikov has been acting lately: "He is morose, gloomy, proud and haughty, and of late—and perhaps for a long time before—he has been suspicious and fanciful. He has a noble nature and a kind heart; he does not like showing his feelings and would rather do a cruel thing than open his heart freely. . .It's as though he were alternating between two characters." These two characters are best represented as his cold, intellectual detached side, which emphasizes power and self-will, and his warm, humane compassionate side, which suggests self-submissiveness and meekness. The intellectual side is a result of his deliberate and premeditated actions; that is, when he is functioning on this side, he never acts spontaneously, but instead, every action is premeditated. It is this aspect of his personality that enables him to formulate his theories about crime and to commit the crime.

In order to emphasize this dual character in Raskolnikov, Dostoevsky created two other characters in the novel who represent the opposing sides of his character. These characters are Sonya and Svidrigailov.

Svidrigailov represents the cold intellectual side that emphasizes self-will. All of Svidrigailov's acts are performed so as to give him pleasure and to place him above common morality. This is not to imply that Svidrigailov is an intellectual, but rather it implies that he does not allow minor human actions, morality, or law to prevent him from having his own way. Thus, as Raskolnikov could commit a murder because of his theories, so can Svidrigailov rape a 15-year-old mute girl for his own gratification.

Raskolnikov's intellectual side is intricately bound up in his theory of the extraordinary man. If Raskolnikov is to be one of the extraordinary, he must be able to stand alone, without needing human companionship or without being influenced by the actions of others. He must rely on no one and must be completely self-sufficient. When he performs charitable acts, he is temporarily violating this intellectual side of his nature.

The other side of Rodya's character is the warm, compassionate side. It operates without an interceding thought process. His first and immediate reaction to any situation represents this aspect of his personality. Consequently, he will often act in a warm, friendly, charitable, or humane manner, and then when he has had a chance to think over his actions intellectually, he regrets them. For instance, when he spontaneously gives Katerina Marmeladov his last money, he regrets that he has given the Marmeladov family the money shortly afterwards. If left to his immediate reactions, Raskolnikov would always act in a charitable and humane manner; he would always sacrifice himself for his fellow man—incidents galore abound in this manner, including the reports of his risking his life to rescue a child from a fire or his concern over a drugged young girl who is being pursued by a "dandy" with immoral intent.

The actions in the novel that seem to be strange and contradictory are rather the result of the two aspects of Raskolnikov's personality. When he refuses to allow Dunya to marry Luzhin and then a moment later tells her to marry whom she pleases, this reversal is an example of the humane side not wanting his sister to sacrifice herself to help him, and then the intellectual side contending that he must not concern himself with insignificant problems of others.

Sonya Semyonovna Marmeladov

Sonya functions in the novel as one aspect of Raskolnikov's character and also as the "passive redemptive" figure. She is the meek and self-submissive figure. Her function is to help redeem Raskolnikov, but her redemptive role is a passive one. This means that she does little in an active way to make Raskolnikov confess or change his way. Rather, she is simply available whenever Raskolnikov needs her. The question arises as to how can she be redemptive: She is redemptive because through her suffering she becomes for Raskolnikov the symbol of all the suffering humanity, that is, all the suffering of mankind is represented in her own suffering. And through her compassionate nature and ability to love, she touches deeply one side of Raskolnikov's character. Her life is one of simple expedience for existence.

No one is less fit for a life of prostitution than is Sonya, but this was the only way in which she could help support her family. She became a prostitute but feels intensely the degradation and shame of her profession. But in spite of this profession, she has never lost touch with God. Her simple faith in God is part of her strength. She attends church as much as possible, has masses said for Lizaveta Ivanovna, and has the basic faith in the goodness of Divine Providence. She also refuses to answer questions put to her by Raskolnikov (that is, who is to live or die) by saying "how can I know God's will?" She could never assert her own will to the degree that the will of Divine Providence would be put into question.

Arkady Svidrigailov

Svidrigailov has one function in life—to satisfy his sensual desires. To do so often takes strange ways and means. He represents a type of "Übermensch," or extraordinary man. This type feels that the world is essentially an evil place; therefore to be in tune with this universe, one must essentially be evil. Since there can be no Divine Providence whose will is stronger than man's, each individual must assert his own will and power. Since the universe is meaningless and directionless, man's main course of action is the complete gratification of the appetite. Therefore, for Svidrigailov, his pleasure and gratification are all that matter. How they are achieved is unimportant. Svidrigailov admits to Raskolnikov that he has a "natural propensity" for the vulgar. He has no scruples about getting his own way. His life has been constructed on the idea that his own feelings and pleasures are more important than anything else; therefore, he can rape a mute 15-year-old girl and, upon hearing that this girl has hanged herself, have no feelings of remorse. He simply shrugs his shoulders.

Of equal importance are Svidrigailov's acts of seeming charity. If he does perform good charitable acts, it is not because he sees the acts as good actions but simply because the impulse of the moment gives him pleasure. Likewise, in his kindness to the Marmeladov family, he is hoping to deceive Raskolnikov and Dunya into believing that he has reformed from his previous evil ways.

At last, even Svidrigailov realizes that he cannot live completely alone and isolated from the rest of humanity. When he realizes that he cannot have Dunya, he is forced to commit suicide. Suicide is the only thing left that he has not willed for himself. His old manner of living has now been denied him by his realization that he can't live alone and there is no new method left to him. Therefore, he takes his life as the only course of action open to him.

Porfiry Petrovitch

Whereas Svidrigailov was working for the gratification of the self, Porfiry is working for the betterment of mankind or, more limited, for the greatness of the Slavic world that needs talented and intelligent young people. Porfiry is a person who believes that Russia is destined to become the great nation of the world and will guide the world into a new era based on love and understanding. Consequently, he feels that any person who has intellectual potential should be serving mother Russia in order to attain these goals. He sees in Raskolnikov a potentially great man who had deceived himself by adhering too much to new and radical intellectual ideas that have come from outside of Russia. Porfiry believes that when Raskolnikov finds his true self, he will then become a man with potential greatness and a man who can do a great service for Russia. If he were to play the part of the average policeman or criminal investigator and concern himself only with trapping the criminal immediately, Porfiry would have arrested Raskolnikov very early in the novel. But Porfiry's aim is not so much to see the criminal locked behind bars as it is to help rehabilitate the criminal and make him into a useful member of society. Therefore, in the final interview, Porfiry gives Raskolnikov some more time in order to confess because a free confession would mitigate the sentence.

Through all of their interviews, Porfiry shows himself to be one of the advanced thinkers of Russia through his use of psychology and new methods, and his belief in the possible rehabilitation of criminals into useful members of society.

CRITICAL ESSAYS

On the pages that follow, the writer of this study guide pro-vides critical scholarship on various aspects of Dostoevsky's *Crime and Punishment*. These interpretive essays are intended solely to enhance your understanding of the original literary work; they are supplemental materials and are not to replace your reading of *Crime and Punishment*. When you're finished reading *Crime and Punishment*, and prior to your reading this study guide's critical essays, consider making a bulleted list of what you think are the most important themes and symbols. Write a short paragraph under each bullet explaining *why* you think that theme or symbol is important; include at least one short quote from the original literary work that supports your contention. Then, test your list and reasons against those found in the following essays. Do you include themes and symbols that the study guide author doesn't? If so, this self test might indicate that you are well on your way to understanding origi-nal literary work. But if not, perhaps you will need to re-read *Crime and Punishment*.

Raskolnikov: A Dual or Split Personality

Prior to this novel, Dostoevsky had used characters whose personalities were dual ones. However, it is not until this novel that he exposes the reader to a full study of the split personality. Raskolnikov's dual personality is the controlling idea behind the murder and behind his punishment. Raskolnikov is used as a representative of the modern young Russian intellectual whose fate is intricately bound up in the fate of Russia herself. Therefore, the story is a parable of the fate of a nihilistic and skeptical youth in nineteenth century Russia, a position once held by Dostoevsky himself, but he later rejected the revolutionary opinions and came to hate and fear them. *Crime and Punishment* was to be a vision of the ultimate error and moral sufferings of those who had so cut themselves off from established authority and morality that they lost all respect for human life. Therefore, the life and aims of Raskolnikov became in some ways the fate of the young Russian intellectuals.

But Dostoevsky loved Raskolnikov. Dostoevsky presents most of the story from Raskolnikov's viewpoint, and most of the actions and most of our views are seen through his eyes. Dostoevsky, as author, seldom leaves Raskolnikov except when, in some short scenes, his thesis demanded attention elsewhere.

The plot of the novel presents a double conflict, one external and one internal: the one conflict between the estranged individual and his hostile universe, the other a clash between an isolated soul and his ethical or aesthetic consciousness. Since the plot is a double conflict, the first general problem is to understand Raskolnikov's dual personality. There are several ways of seeing this. In its broadest view, Raskolnikov fluctuates between the ideas of complete self-will and power, and extreme meekness and self-submissiveness.

Actions in the novel that seem to be contradictory are a result of Raskolnikov's fluctuation between these two extremes of his personality; therefore, the first part of the novel deals with a crime committed by this young intellectual. The crime was a result of a theory he conceived about the nature of man's abilities; that is, some have abilities which make them extraordinary while other possess no abilities. It was this intellectual aspect of his character that causes him to conceive and execute his crime. He wants to see if he had the daring to transcend conscience. His punishment comes about as a result of the transcendence of conscience. Therefore, one aspect of his character is a cold, inhumane, detached intellectuality which emphasizes the individual power and self-will. The other aspect is the warm, compassionate side, revealed in his charitable acts and his reluctance to accept praise or credit.

The problem in the novel, therefore, is to bring these two opposing parts of Raskolnikov's personality into a single functioning person. To do this, Dostoevsky opens with the crime, which is handled rather quickly so as to get to the punishment. The murder is symbolic of Raskolnikov's thinking. It is the result of having cut himself off from authority, from love, and from mankind.

The Redemptive Characters: Sonya and Porfiry

In spite of his crime, Raskolnikov is worth redeeming and therefore since Raskolnikov is a dual personality, Dostoevsky also felt the need of creating two additional characters who, taken separately, represent the two opposing aspects of his nature. Thus, Sonya is the warm human, compassionate, charitable aspect of Raskolnikov's character. She is the meek and submissive personality. She will become the symbol of "the suffering of all humanity."

In contrast Svidrigailov is the detached cold manifestation of the self-will and power and intellect. Consequently, so often in the novel, when Raskolnikov is attracted to Sonya, he is repulsed by the depravity of Svidrigailov. Likewise, when he is talking or going to see Svidrigailov, he is disgusted with and repulsed by Sonya's tears and weaknesses.

With Raskolnikov's character established as a dual one, and with these two characters, Sonya and Svidrigailov, representing the two alternating aspects, the general pattern of the novel is to bring Raskolnikov back into one functioning character. Thus, we must have two redemptive characters. Here the importance of Sonya's role is seen. As she represents one aspect of Raskolnikov's personality, so must she function as the person who is to redeem that aspect. Therefore, Sonya is the redemptive figure for Raskolnikov's humane aspect of his personality. Through her suffering, she makes him realize the importance of a love for humanity, that a human being cannot be "a louse" or a parasite sucking the life from other human beings. But it should be emphasized that

Sonya does not accomplish her purpose by overt action. She is the passive figure whose simple presence is enough to inspire Raskolnikov's actions.

The other redemptive figure is Porfiry. Here is an intellectual man who uses his intellect for the good of man. He sees in Raskolnikov the potential of a great being who made up a theory and then was ashamed that it broke down. Porfiry is the man who recognizes that the theory is base but that Raskolnikov is far from being base. His purpose, therefore, is to make Raskolnikov see the difference between the baseness of the theory and the ever-present potential in himself. What Porfiry realizes is that any idea, if it is conceived of for the benefit of humanity, must be a human idea and must be executed by a humane person. He tries to make Raskolnikov see that the idea is base because it views a large portion of mankind as base.

Thus Raskolnikov at the beginning of the novel is a dual personality with two aspects of his personality represented by Sonya and Svidrigailov. The problem is to bring this personality into an integrated whole. This task is assigned to Sonya and Porfiry. The emphasis is that man cannot separate the humane aspect of his life from the intellectual aspect. Whatever man does must be done in terms of the betterment of general humanity.

Raskolnikov's punishment, that is the general suffering he undergoes, is a result of this split personality. It was one aspect that murdered the old pawnbroker, but it is the humane side that must suffer for the murder.

The Ubermensch or Extraordinary Man Theories

Raskolnikov's theories about the ordinary man versus the extraordinary man are often blurred and indistinct in his own mind. If one is to assume that the crime was committed in order to prove a theory, then the flaws in the crime indicate the flaws or incompleteness of the theory.

If the theories seem to be contradictory at times, it is not a result of Dostoevsky's carelessness; quite the contrary, Dostoevsky intentionally made the theory contradictory at times. Raskolnikov had to commit the murder before he had completely formulated the theory. Dostoevsky wanted to show the young intellectual being influenced by various theories and then using these theories before he had had a chance to analyze them. For example, a typical contradiction would be that Raskolnikov will at one time maintain that the murder was committed to benefit mankind, but then he will maintain that the extraordinary man must be above mankind and not be concerned with what mankind will think of him. Such an incomplete understanding of his own thoughts and such contradictory statements are the rationale that leads Raskolnikov to the possibility of redemption. A brief analysis of the various ideas will partly show what aspect of the theories are borrowed and what aspects are the result of Raskolnikov's own thinking.

The German philosopher Georg Wilhelm Friedrich Hegel (1770-1830) wrote many works on the general nature of the Ubermensch or extraordinary man. His ideas, however, were never formulated into one consistent thesis. But generally extracted from various parts of his philosophy, his views may be stated with some consistency. In its broadest statement, the Hegelian man exists for noble purposes; if the ends are noble, then the means can be justified. The emphasis is always on the *ends* rather than the *means*. As applied to Raskolnikov's crime, the theories have relevance in the following ways.

The old pawnbroker is an evil person who is actually harming the poor people who come to her for pawning. According to Hegel, any harmful segment of society should be removed. Therefore, Raskolnikov reasons that by murdering the old pawnbroker, he will be removing a harmful "louse" from society.

If the ends are noble, the means can be justified. The old pawnbroker has a lot of money that will be "wasted" upon useless requiem services for her soul after her death. With that money, Raskolnikov will be able to complete his education and devote himself to the service of humanity, or he could distribute the money among needy and starving families, thus saving hundreds of people from ruin and destitution.

Dostoevsky had also apparently encountered other views of the Superman or Ubermensch—views that were not yet formulated in any coherent whole but were heard wherever intellectuals gathered. Svidrigailov was born from these ideas of self-gratification. Svidrigailov would reason: Since there is no will (or power) beyond that of my own, I must completely assert my own will until it is totally free of all restraint against it. Since there is no power beyond me that functions to punish, I am free to assert completely my own will.

Therefore, the Svidrigailov type of Ubermensch is one who possesses the strongest will and is able to make his desires and his power dominant over others. Svidrigailov can rape a 15-year-old girl and cause the death of a servant without any fear of punishment. He asserts his own will in order to gratify his own desires.

The test of this type of Ubermensch is that he must stand completely alone and must not allow his will to be influenced by the wishes of others. Thus, this assertion of the will isolates man from society. When Raskolnikov attempts to assert his will, he finds himself cut off from the rest of humanity. It is this dreadful solitude that Raskolnikov cannot stand and that makes him confess to become part of humanity again.

Raskolnikov's own theory adopts some of all of the above ideas with certain touches of his own. For Raskolnikov, all men are divided into two categories: ordinary and extraordinary. The ordinary man has to live in submission and has no right to transgress the law because he is ordinary. On the contrary, the extraordinary men have the right to commit any crime and to transgress the law in any way. They are extraordinary because they are the men who have the gift or talent to utter a *New Word*. It is the extraordinary men who forge civilization onward to new heights of achievements. The extraordinary man has this inner right to decide whether to overstep the law or any obstacle that stands in the way of the practical fulfillment of his idea, or New Words.

All great men capable of giving something new to society must not submit to the common law because if they do they cease to be great. Great men create new laws by their discoveries and therefore should have the right to eliminate a few men in order to make their new discoveries known to all of humanity. Thus, Raskolnikov "sanctions bloodshed in the name of conscience." (Raskolnikov constantly refers to Napoleon because Napoleon had the daring to commit various acts in order to complete his plans.)

Again it should be emphasized that, at the time of the murder, Raskolnikov had not worked these various theories into a consistent whole. All the individual parts were there, but some of the connecting details were missing. The murder was committed to see whether he dares commit a murder and therefore proves his will is strong.

CliffsNotes Review

Fill in the Blanks

1. What is Rodion (Rodya) and Dunya's Patronymic? Rodion_____; Dunya_____.

2. Roskolnikov believes that Porfiry is playing a game of _____.

3. The Yellow Card that Sonya carries indicates that she is a licensed _____.

4. For Raskolnikov, the perfect example of the Ubermensch [Superman] is _____.

5. Raskolnikov is attracted to Sonya because she is the perfect example of _____.

6. Raskolnikov's alter ego is best represented by _____.

7. Raskolnikov murders both _____ and her half sister _____.

8. At his confession, Raskolnikov picks up the Bible and asks Sonya to read _____.

9. After his trial, Raskolnikov is sent to _____.

10. Raskolnikov receives a relatively light sentence of _____ years.

Answers: (1) Rodion Romanovitch and Dunya Romanovna (2) cat and mouse (3) Prostitute (4) Napoleon (5) "the suffering of all Humanity" (6) Svidrigailov (7) Alyona [Alena]; Lizaveta (8) The Raising of Lazarus (9) Siberia (10) eight

Identify the Quote: Find Each Quote in *Crime and Punishment*

1. "Does not my heart bleed because I am an abject and useless creature. . .do you know what it is to so plead without hope. . .to have nobody else, no other place to turn to, . . .to be absolutely alone. . .dare you, looking upon me at this moment, say, with conviction that I am not a swine?"

2. Any man who has any [conscience] must suffer if he is conscious of error . . . .Suffering and pain are always obligatory on those of wide intellect and profound feeling. Truly great men must, I think, experience great sorrow on the earth.

3. "Well, didn't I say we had something in common . .Wasn't I right when I said we were kindred spirits. . .I am indeed idle and depraved. . .but I keep fancying there is something very like me in you."

4. "Go at once, this instant, stand at the cross-roads, first bow down and kiss the earth you have desecrated, then bow to the whole world. . .and say aloud to all the . . . four corners of the earth and say to all the world 'I have done murder.'"

5. "It was I who killed the old woman and her sister, Lizaveta, with an axe and robbed them."

Answers: (1) Marmeladov to Raskolnikov at their first meeting in the bar. (2) Raskolnikov to Porfiry when questioned about his theories of the ubermensch. (3) Svidrigailov to Raskolnikov, reminding him that they have something in common. (4) Sonya to Raskolnikov after his confession. (5) Raskolnikov's confession to the police officials at the end of the book.

Essay Questions

1. What concepts of Law are prominent in *Crime and Punishment*? What new legal techniques and psychological methods does Porfiry employ?

2. What concepts of Christianity are prominent in *Crime and Punishment*? Why didn't Raskolnikov read the story of Lazarus himself or why did he ask Sonya to read it to him?

3. Discuss briefly the rationale by which Raskolnikov considers himself a superior man.

4. What are the laws governing the extraordinary man?

5. How might Raskolnikov answer the objection that his theory is only an attempt to justify unrestrained self-will?

6. How does Dostoevsky forestall the reader's assumption that his central character is simply mad?

7. How is Svidrigailov shown to represent one aspect of Raskolnikov's character?

8. When Raskolnikov is with Svidrigailov, what repulses him about the man?

9. What attracts Raskolnikov, the intellectual, to the simple and uneducated Sonya?

10. Why does Svidrigailov commit suicide?

11. How do dreams function in the novel?

12. What is the function of the Epilogue?

Practice Projects

1. Consider the proposition that fundamentally Raskolnikov progresses from the adherence to theory and ignorance of self to knowledge of self and rejection of theory.

2. What does Dostoevsky gain artistically by representing Sonya as a prostitute? What biblical character did he likely have in mind?

3. Choose the incidents that seem to be major crises in Raskolnikov's life and determine what each contributes to his development.

4. What irony and value are there in making Sonya the principal outside agent of Raskolnikov's redemption?

5. The structure of the novel allows Raskolnikov to have alternate interviews with Sonya and Svidrigailov. Discuss the relationship of these two characters to Raskolnikov.

CliffsNotes Resource Center

The learning doesn't need to stop here. CliffsNotes Resource Center shows you the best of the best—links to the best information in print and online about the author and/or related works. And don't think that this is all we've prepared for you; we've put all kinds of pertinent information at www.cliffsnotes.com. Look for all the terrific resources at your favorite bookstore or local library and on the Internet. When you're online, make your first stop www.cliffsnotes.com where you'll find more incredibly useful information about *Crime and Punishment*.

Books

This CliffsNotes book provides a meaningful interpretation of *Crime and Punishment* by Wiley Publishing, Inc. If you are looking for more information about the author and/or related works, check out these other publications:

"Crime and Punishment: A Study of Dostoevsky," by R. P. Blackmur, is an old article, yet it has been reprinted so often that it is worth consideration. The author was one of the signficant critics of mid-twentieth century. Chimera, 1943.

Dostoevsky: The Miraculous Years, 1865-1871, by Joseph Frank, represents the most definitive and detailed account of Dostoevsky's life and publications. The second volume concerns itself with the period during which *Crime and Punishment* was written. Princeton, 1995.

Dialogues with Dostoevsky: The Overwhelming Questions, by Robert L. Jakson, is one of the most extensive studies in recent years by a well known authority of Dostoevsky. This book relates Dostoevsky's ideas to those found in Turgenev, Tolstoy, Checkhov, Gorki, and other Russian writers. This is a must for students interested in the large picture of Russian literature from mid-nineteenth century to the present. Stanford Univerity Press, 1993.

Dostoevsky's Fantastic Realism, by Malcohm V. Tones, discusses Dostoevsky's untenable position in relation to Raskolnikov and his extensive use of the psychological concept of "objectification" and "subjectivity," showing how Raskolnikov objectifies his murder and subjectively accepts his punishment. Cambridge University Press, 1990.

Dostoevsky: The Art of Integral Vision, by Martrina Kostalevshy. Raskolnikov's punishment should consider the agonies of fear, spite, and despair in which Raskolnikov finds himself after committing his crime. New Haven & London: Yale Univeristy Press, 1997.

Dostoevsky on Evil and Atonement: The Ontology of Personalism in His Major Fiction, by Linda Kraeger & Joe Barnhart. This work discusses Dostoevsky's views on Utilitarianism and John Stuart Mill's Principles. See especially pp. 138-141. See also the critique of the Napolionic Ideas, pp. 141-144. Wales: The Edwin Mellen Press, 1992.

Dostoevsky, The Making of a Novelist, by Ernest J. Simmons. Professor Simmons almost single-handedly brought Russian literature to the broad attention of the American reading public and academic circles. His early study stands today as a landmark in Dostoevsky criticism. London: Oxford, 1950.

The Notebooks for Crime and Punishment, by Edward Wasiolek and trans., is invaluable for a student. All of the various ideas of the novel are sketched and some are developed, and some are modified and discarded. Chicago: University Press, 1967.

It's easy to find books published by Wiley Publishing, Inc. You'll find them in your favorite bookstores (on the Internet and at a store near you). We also have three Web sites that you can use to read about all the books we publish:

■ www.cliffsnotes.com
■ www.dummies.com
■ www.wiley.com

Internet

Check out these Web resources for more information about Fyodor Dostoevsky and *Crime and Punishment*:

SparkNotes: Online Study Guides, http://www.sparknotes.com/guides/crime/ — Commentary and discussion of Dostoevsky's Crime and Punishment.

Index of Dostoevsky from Middlebury College, http://www.middlebury.edu/~beyer/courses/previous/ru351/dostoevsky/F.M.Dostoevsky.shtml — Essays, reading guides, and explications of character relationships and themes.

Christiaan Stange's Dostoevsky Research Station, http://www.kiosek.com/dostoevsky/ — Compact, reliable site for information about Dostoevsky and his works.

Crime and Punishment Essay, http://www.halfaya.org/leo/writing/story/crime.html — Radical, thought-provoking essay concerning the pivotal murder of the old pawnbroker in *Crime and Punishment*.

Western Canon Great Books University, http:// www.westerncanon.com/cgibin/lecture/Dostoevskyhall/wwwboard.html — Write in Dostoevsky "Crime+and+punishment" and click Search. Provides a rich source of research bibliographical material.

Films

Crime and Punishment, Columbia Classics, 1935. A 8MM film directed by Josef Von Sternberg. A very low budget film saved in part by the imaginative direction of Sternberg. Stars Edward Arnold as Raskolnikov and Peter Lorre as Porfiry.

Crime and Punishment, 1959. USA. This version is directed by Denis Sanders and stars George Hamilton in his film debut as the darkly handsome Raskolnikov. At variance in many ways with the novel.

Send Us Your Favorite Tips

In your quest for knowledge, have you ever experienced that sublime moment when you figure out a trick that saves time or trouble? Perhaps you realized you were taking ten steps to accomplish something that could have taken two. Or you found a little-known workaround that achieved great results. If you've discovered a useful tip that helped you regain information more effectively and you'd like to share it, the CliffsNotes staff would love to hear from you. Go to our Web site at www.cliffsnotes.com and click the Talk to Us button. If we select your tip, we may publish it as part of CliffsNotes Daily, our exciting, free e-mail newsletter. To find out more or to subscribe to a newsletter, go to www.cliffsnotes.com on the Web.

Street Map

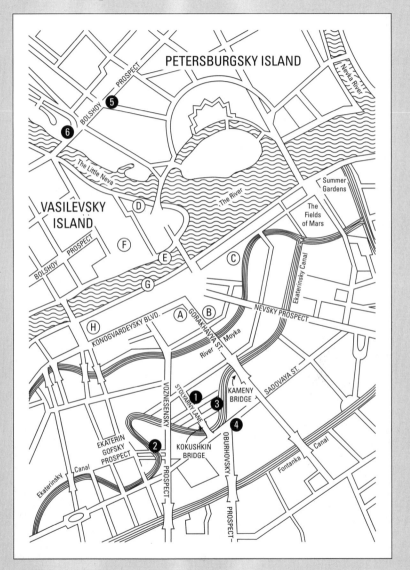

Places of Importance in Crime and Punishment

1. Raskolnikov's room located in the slums of St. Petersburg.

2. The pawnbroker's room: The distance as counted by Raskolnikov was 730 paces. Curious critics have since walked the distance between the two buildings and found that it was indeed about 730 paces.

3. Sonya's room: Note that it is only a short distance from Raskolnikov's room.

4. Hay Market Square: This is undoubtedly where Sonya plied her trade and where Raskolnikov bows and kisses the earth.

5. Place of Svidrigailov's suicide: Note that he is some distance from his room, which was next to Sonya's.

6. Tuchkov Bridge: This is probably where Raskolnikov contemplated suicide until he saw the woman jump over.

Important Landmarks in St. Petersburg

A. Saint Isaac's Cathedral: For the orthodox Russian, this magnificent cathedral is the equivalent to St. Peter's Basillica in Rome.

B. The Admiralty Building

C. The Winter Palace and the Ermitage: This is the residence of the Tsar when he is in St. Petersburg. Today the Ermitage houses one of the greatest art collections in the world.

D. The Stock Exchange

E. Academy of Sciences

F. The university where Raskolnikov once attended. It later was named Leningrad University.

G. The famous statue to Peter the Great.

H. The Senate.

Index

CliffsNotes

LITERATURE NOTES

CliffsN☉tes™

The Odyssey
Oedipus Trilogy
Of Human Bondage
Of Mice and Men
The Old Man and
    the Sea
Old Testament
Oliver Twist
The Once and
    Future King
One Day in the Life of
    Ivan Denisovich
One Flew Over
    the Cuckoo's Nest
100 Years of Solitude
O'Neill's Plays
Othello
Our Town
The Outsiders
The Ox Bow Incident
Paradise Lost
A Passage to India
The Pearl
The Pickwick Papers
The Picture of
    Dorian Gray
Pilgrim's Progress
The Plague
Plato's Euthyphro…
Plato's The Republic
Poe's Short Stories
A Portrait of the
    Artist…
The Portrait of a Lady
The Power and
    the Glory
Pride and Prejudice
The Prince
The Prince and
    the Pauper
A Raisin in the Sun
The Red Badge of
    Courage
The Red Pony
The Return of the
    Native
Richard II
Richard III

The Rise of
    Silas Lapham
Robinson Crusoe
Roman Classics
Romeo and Juliet
The Scarlet Letter
A Separate Peace
Shakespeare's
    Comedies
Shakespeare's Histories
Shakespeare's
    Minor Plays
Shakespeare's Sonnets
Shakespeare's Tragedies
Shaw's Pygmalion &
    Arms…
Silas Marner
Sir Gawain…Green
    Knight
Sister Carrie
Slaughterhouse-five
Snow Falling on Cedars
Song of Solomon
Sons and Lovers
The Sound and the Fury
Steppenwolf &
    Siddhartha
The Stranger
The Sun Also Rises
T.S. Eliot's Poems &
    Plays
A Tale of Two Cities
The Taming of the
    Shrew
Tartuffe, Misanthrope…
The Tempest
Tender Is the Night
Tess of the D'Urbervilles
Their Eyes Were
    Watching God
Things Fall Apart
The Three Musketeers
To Kill a Mockingbird
Tom Jones
Tom Sawyer
Treasure Island &
    Kidnapped
The Trial

Tristram Shandy
Troilus and Cressida
Twelfth Night
Ulysses
Uncle Tom's Cabin
The Unvanquished
Utopia
Vanity Fair
Vonnegut's Works
Waiting for Godot
Walden
Walden Two
War and Peace
Who's Afraid of
    Virginia…
Winesburg, Ohio
The Winter's Tale
The Woman Warrior
Worldly Philosophers
Wuthering Heights
A Yellow Raft in
    Blue Water

Check Out the All-New CliffsNotes Guides

TECHNOLOGY TOPICS
Balancing Your Check-
    book with Quicken
Buying and Selling
    on eBay™
Buying Your First PC
Creating a Winning
    PowerPoint 2000
    Presentation
Creating Web Pages
    with HTML
Creating Your First
    Web Page
Exploring the World
    with Yahoo!
Getting on the Internet
Going Online with AOL
Making Windows 98
    Work for You

Setting Up a
    Windows 98
    Home Network
Shopping Online Safel⟨
Upgrading and
    Repairing Your PC
Using Your First iMac⟨
Using Your First PC
Writing Your First
    Computer Program

PERSONAL FINANCE TOPICS
Budgeting & Saving
    Your Money
Getting a Loan
Getting Out of Debt
Investing for the
    First Time
Investing in
    401(k) Plans
Investing in IRAs
Investing in
    Mutual Funds
Investing in the
    Stock Market
Managing Your Mone⟨
Planning Your
    Retirement
Understanding
    Health Insurance
Understanding
    Life Insurance

CAREER TOPICS
Delivering a Winning
    Job Interview
Finding a Job
    on the Web
Getting a Job
Writing a Great Resum⟨